Praise for James Chambers'
Palmerston: The People's Darling

'Superb'
Andrew Roberts, *The Times*

'A rollicking biography, weaving raunch with realpolitik, told with the bold swagger of Palmerston himself'
Simon Sebag Montefiore, *Daily Telegraph*

'In his well-written and highly readable account, James Chambers gives us full measure on Palmerston the man as well as the politician. An excellent introduction to the great man'
Frank McLynn, *Independent on Sunday*

'Elegant, ironic… even those who would not normally read political biography will enjoy this one for the quality of its writing and the exuberance of its hero'
Andrew Roberts, *Sunday Telegraph*

'Wonderfully fresh and fluent… Chambers' is, in the best sense, a sensibly revisionist life'
Nigel Jones, *Literary Review*

'Accessible, entertaining biography… to be welcomed for bringing its subject's colourful character, and the Victorian world in which it operated, to life'
Tristram Hunt, *BBC History – Books of the Year*

'Chambers handles all the strands with great clarity, he is vivid without being lurid, and this is a superb book'
Robbie Hudson, *Sunday Times*

Chambers shows an admirable grasp of the political scene and the part which Palmerston played in world politics. He writes well, conveying the jauntiness, cheek and trickery of Palmerston's character'
Sarah Bradford, *Evening Standard*

'Engaging biography... Chambers captures the puckish personality of the man and his aristocratic, irreverent, often louche milieu'
Sunday Times

'A long overdue biography written with great élan'
Daily Echo

Charlotte & Leopold

The True Story of the Original People's Princess

JAMES CHAMBERS

Old St PUBLISHING

First published in the United Kingdom in 2007 by
Old Street Publishing Ltd,
28–32 Bowling Green Lane, London EC1R 0BJ
www.oldstreetpublishing.co.uk

ISBN-13: 978 1905847 23 5

10 9 8 7 6 5 4 3 2

Printed by Cromwell Press Limited, Trowbridge, Wiltshire.

For Josephine

Contents

I would like to express my deepest gratitude to Charlie Viney, Ben Yarde-Buller, Sam Carter, Francesca Yarde-Buller, Dr Stephen Steinberg, Ben Illis and Emily Carter. Without their encouragement, enthusiasm and help it would not have been possible to tell this story.

James Chambers
London 2007

'Daughter of England'

———

No one knows better than a medical man how to kill himself. Sir Richard Croft did it very neatly. He slouched in a
tall wing chair and put a pistol in his mouth. When he pulled the
trigger, his blood and brains were caught by the back of the chair.
Only the bullet tore on through into the wall.

For the last three months, the tall, grey, dignified and normally
over-confident Sir Richard had been suffering from serious depression. So what he did was hardly a surprise to anyone. Yet, even so, it
must have seemed selfishly melodramatic to do it in someone else's
house rather than in the privacy of his own.

Despite his imposing manner, Sir Richard was not an eminent or
even qualified physician. He was merely the most fashionable of the
many accoucheurs, or 'men-midwives', who practised in England at
the beginning of the nineteenth century, and his title was an inherited baronetcy rather than a well-earned knighthood. On the day of
his death he was attending a patient, the wife of a rich clergyman,
who was about to give birth in their large house in London's Harley Street. After a preliminary examination, he had as usual left his

patient alone with her husband and gone downstairs to wait for the next contractions. Shown by a servant into the study, he had selected a book, and somehow, unusually in the house of a clergyman, he had discovered a case with pistols in it.

Soon afterwards, when the crump of exploding black powder brought the vicar and his servants running, they found that Sir Richard had died instantly. The pistol had fallen from his right hand onto the floor, and the book, Shakespeare's *Love's Labour's Lost*, was lying on the table beside him beneath his limp left hand. It was open at the point towards the end of Act V, Scene II, where the King of Navarre asks,

'Fair Sir, God save you! Where is the Princess?'

It was, said the coroner, 'a singular coincidence'.

The princess whose whereabouts were the obvious cause of Sir Richard's remorse was another of his patients, Princess Charlotte Augusta of Wales and Saxe-Coburg, and for the last three months she had been lying in her tomb at Windsor with the stillborn son whom she had survived for only five hours.

Her father, the Prince Regent, had written to Sir Richard to reassure him of his 'entire confidence in the medical skill and ability which he displayed during the arduous and protracted labour'. But if the Prince Regent meant what he said, there was not a man or a woman in the kingdom who agreed with him. Their Princess was dead. There was no one to replace her. The nation's heart was broken, and Sir Richard Croft was the only man who could be blamed for it.

On the day after Princess Charlotte's death the leader in *The Times* proclaimed clumsily, 'We never recollect so strong and general an expression and indication of sorrow.' The wife of the Russian Ambassador, the famously libidinous Princess Lieven, put it much better: 'One met in the streets people of every class in tears, the churches full at all hours, the shops shut for a fortnight (an eloquent testimony from a shop-keeping community), and everyone, from the highest to the lowest, in a state of despair which it is impossible to describe.'

Many years later in his memoirs, the Lord Chancellor, Lord Brougham, wrote, 'It really was as though every household throughout Great Britain had lost a favourite child.'

Princess Charlotte had been the most popular member of the royal family. Indeed, for most of her short life she had been the only popular member of it. When she was born, on 7 January 1796, the poet Leigh Hunt, not at his best, wrote, 'Such a fine young royal creature – Daughter of England!' When she died, little more than twenty-one years later, another poet, Thomas Campbell, echoed Hunt's words in an equally unremarkable dirge, which was performed to packed houses by Sarah Bartley at the new Drury Lane Theatre:

> 'Daughter of England! for a nation's sighs,
> A nation's heart went with thine obsequies.'

By the time the costly war with Napoleon was over, the Daughter of England had become a symbol of hope. The reputation of the royal family still stood lower than it had for centuries. But eager, warm-hearted, unpretentious Charlotte was a happy and auspicious contrast to her dissolute father, her variously ineffectual or 'wicked' uncles and her sad, mad grandfather. Because of her, the future seemed more secure. Old King George III was bound to die soon, and the Prince Regent had wrecked his own health so much that he was unlikely to outlive him for long. Until the dreadful news broke on 7 November 1817, everyone in the now disconsolate kingdom had been looking forward to the not-too-distant day when young Queen Charlotte would ascend the throne.

'She would have behaved well', said the Duke of Wellington, 'her death is one of the most serious misfortunes the country has ever met with'.

CHAPTER ONE

'The Brunswick Bride'

———

FOR CHARLOTTE TO have grown up worthy of the Duke of Wellington's compliment was very nearly a miracle. She had emerged confident and merry from a childhood that would have turned almost anyone else into a suspicious recluse. She had never known the security of family life. Instead, her little world, like the great world beyond it, had been a world of conflict and duplicity. From the day she was born until the day she was married, she had seldom been anything but a victim. Her tutors and governesses had misrepresented her whenever it suited them in the course of their vindictive little rivalries. The leaders of the opposition had manipulated her cynically in their political manoeuvring. Worst of all, her own parents, whom she hardly ever saw, had used her as the principal pawn in their embarrassingly public squabbles.

Charlotte's father only married her mother for money – not because Princess Caroline of Brunswick was rich, but because the Prime Minister, William Pitt, had told him that, when he married, the government would raise his income. The increase was intended to cover the cost of an appropriately enlarged household, but to the Prince it was an opportunity to continue his notorious extravagance.

He longed to be regarded as the leader of fashion, the nation's foremost sportsman and the most eminent connoisseur of art and architecture. To that end, he had squandered absurd sums on clothes and horses, and he had lavished fortunes on building and embellishing his pavilion in Brighton and his home in London, Carlton House, each of which he had crammed with an indiscriminate clutter of both exquisite and tasteless pictures and furniture. By 1794, when it was suggested that he should get married, he was hopelessly in debt.

Many of the 'beaux' and 'bucks' who called themselves his friends were almost as extravagant as he was. A few of them had reduced themselves to penury on no more than the turn of a card. But these men had property to sell or pledge for credit. Charlotte's father did not. As Prince of Wales and heir to the throne he had an annual allowance of £60,000 from the privy purse, and as Duke of Cornwall he had an income of £13,000 a year from his duchy. That was all, and by 1794 it was no longer even enough to cover his cost of living, let alone pay the interest on a debt of over £600,000. His desperate creditors had petitioned the Prime Minister for help, but the government, which had bailed him out once already, had no intention of doing so again.

A suitable marriage was the Prince's only hope. The promised increase would raise his allowance from the privy purse to £100,000 a year. Although, in itself, even this would not be enough to support all his extravagance, it would at least enable him to start making annual payments to some of his creditors, and that in turn might encourage others to lend him more. He was unmoved when he was told that it was his duty to get married and provide the kingdom with an heir. But when he was told that a marriage would bring in more money, he agreed at once.

There was still one small problem, however. By his own admision,

His Royal Highness was already married. Nine years earlier, when he was only twenty-three, he had been secretly married to an older woman, a beautiful widow called Maria Fitzherbert. When the King and his Cabinet recovered from the initial shock of this news, they learned to their relief that it was not the impediment it might have been. In the opinion of the Lord Chancellor and the Attorney General, and with the reluctant concurrence of the Archbishop of Canterbury, the marriage was undoubtedly null and void. Since Mrs Fitzherbert was a Roman Catholic it was forbidden by the Bill of Rights of 1689 and the Act of Settlement of 1700, and since the Prince had married without his father's permission, it was also in breach of the Royal Marriages Act of 1772.

The Prince was genuinely fond of Mrs Fitzherbert. But he was not so fond as to be faithful. He had recently acquired a mistress, the beautiful but sinister Lady Jersey, who was almost ten years his senior (even older than Mrs Fitzherbert). And he was not *so* fond of anyone as to allow them to stand between him and an opportunity to increase his income. The news that he was not legally married was as much of a relief to the Prince as it was to the government.

Once it was agreed that the Prince was free to marry, the next step was to find him a bride. There were two candidates, both of whom were his cousins. One was Princess Louise of Mecklenburg-Strelitz, whose father was the brother of his mother, Queen Charlotte. The other was Princess Caroline of Brunswick, whose mother was a sister of his father, the King.

The Queen was enthusiastically in favour of Princess Louise, not only because Louise was her niece and reputedly the better looking, but also because, like many other people at court, she had heard too many unsavoury rumours about Princess Caroline. The Brunswicker Princess was said to be coarse and uninhibited. She was said to have had several affairs, one with an Irish officer in her father's army, and it was known that earlier marriage negotiations had been broken off without reason.

But the woman who had the most influence over the Prince of Wales, Lady Jersey, was equally enthusiastic in her support for Princess Caroline. Lady Jersey had managed to replace Mrs Fitzherbert in the Prince's bed, but she had not succeeded in replacing her in his heart. Now that good fortune had come to her aid and removed Mrs Fitzherbert from the stage altogether, Lady Jersey was determined to ensure that the next wife should be the least formidable rival; if only half the stories were true, Princess Caroline was certainly that.

Naturally the Prince was persuaded by Lady Jersey. Yet even after he had plumped for Princess Caroline, his mother made no secret of her continuing disapproval. From all that she was saying, it was obvious that she was going to make her daughter-in-law's life as difficult as she could – and she clearly realised what Lady Jersey was up to. Applying the old adage 'my enemy's enemy is my friend', she invited Lady Jersey to visit her regularly at Windsor. She lobbied everyone at court on Lady Jersey's behalf, recommending her for a position in the Prince's new household. In the end she succeeded. At the insistence of the mischievous old Queen, her son's mistress was appointed to serve as lady-in-waiting to his wife.

❋

So a heartbroken but dignified Mrs Fitzherbert retired to a beautiful villa by the Thames at Twickenham, Marble Hill, and the greatest British diplomat of the age, James Harris, who had been created Baron Malmesbury six years earlier, was instructed to go to Brunswick and escort Princess Caroline to England.

Malmesbury was in King George's electorate of Hanover when he received his orders. He had gone there to rest after visiting Berlin, where he had used the promise of huge British subsidies to persuade the King of Prussia to keep his army on a war footing along the north bank of the Rhine.

Ever since the outbreak of the French Revolution, Pitt had been using British money to bind the rest of Europe together in a coalition against the new republic. At the outset he had even managed to persuade the Prussians to go on the offensive. In 1792, after the French imprisoned their royal family, the Prussians had sent an army south across the Rhine, commanded by none other than Princess Caroline's father, the Duke of Brunswick.

When he reached Valmy, Brunswick was halted by an artillery barrage. It cost him only a few hundred men and should not have delayed him for long. But in the days that followed he lost thousands more to dysentery and was forced to march back into Prussia.

Meanwhile, further west, it was the French who went on the offensive. They invaded and occupied Belgium, which was then known as the Austrian Netherlands. But in the following year, shortly after they had guillotined their King, the French were routed at Neerwinden by an Austrian army, which was mostly paid with British money and was commanded by the brilliant Prince Frederick, the younger son of the Duke of Coburg. It was said in Paris at the time that the greatest enemies of the Revolution were Coburg and Pitt.

A few days after the battle twenty thousand British soldiers landed in Holland commanded by their King's second son, the Duke of York. The Duke joined forces with a small Dutch army led by the two sons of the Prince of Orange, and together they put themselves under the overall command of Prince Frederick.

At first Prince Frederick's success continued. The allies invaded France. The remnants of the French army faded away ahead of them. The road to Paris lay open. The city was undefended. It was one of the great lost opportunities of history. If the Princes of the Houses of Hanover, Orange and Saxe-Coburg had only been allowed to advance on the capital, the French monarchy might have been restored, Europe might have been spared the terrible war that ravaged it for the next twenty years, and Napoleon Bonaparte might have had nothing better to do with his life than accept the Ottoman

Emperor's invitation to go east and take command of his artillery.

But the allies did not advance. The British and Austrian governments diverted their armies onto much more trivial objectives – the British merely wanted to make a gesture and recapture Calais, which had been lost to the French during the reign of Bloody Mary over two hundred years earlier.

The new rulers of France were given time to recover. While they eliminated their internal enemies in the wanton slaughter that became known as 'the Terror', they introduced conscription and spent all the money they could raise on artillery. A few months later they returned to the offensive. Relying entirely on firepower, force of numbers and a cruel disdain for casualties, they defeated the allies and forced them to retreat. While Malmesbury was negotiating in Berlin, British soldiers were falling back through Holland.

Malmesbury was lucky to be in Hanover when he received his orders. He had only to cross the eastern border to be in Brunswick. If he had gone out from England, he would have had to choose between travelling on the direct route through Holland, which would have meant crossing a war zone, or else sailing north on the safe but much longer route round it.

He reached Brunswick on 20 November and was 'much embarrassed' on being presented to Princess Caroline. It was clear from the dishevelled state of her clothes that no one had helped her to dress and that no one had ever taught her how to do it herself; it was also obvious for other reasons that it was at least several days since she had washed herself. The great Ambassador's report on what he saw was more matter-of-fact than diplomatic. 'Pretty face – not expressive of softness – her figure not graceful – fine eyes – good hands – tolerable teeth but going – fair hair and light eyebrows, good bust...'

The Duke of Brunswick was much more interested in the progress of the war than in his daughter's impending marriage. But he was concerned enough to take Malmesbury aside one evening after supper and give him what he thought was an honest assessment of her. 'She is no fool', he said, 'but she lacks judgement'.

It was an understatement. Twenty-six-year-old Princess Caroline did nothing discreetly. She was over-familiar with everyone, and her conversation was coarse and tactless. During his stay in Brunswick, Malmesbury spent most of his time teaching her manners, dignity and discretion.

They left for England on 29 December. On orders from London, they took the shortest route, expecting to meet up with the British squadron which, they were told, would be waiting for them off the coast of Holland. But when they came close to the Dutch border Malmesbury received a letter from General Harcourt, who had replaced the Duke of York as commander of the British army. Harcourt warned him that it was too dangerous to continue. The British were still retreating. If he tried to reach the coast now, he would have to pass through the French lines to do it. Despite the Princess's insistence that she was a Brunswicker and not afraid, Malmesbury took her back as far as Osnabruck, where they waited eagerly for news of a reversal of fortune for the allies.

But the news, when it came, towards the end of the month, was not what they wanted to hear. The French were now in control of Holland, and they were already so sure of keeping control that they were preparing to make radical changes. Although the United Provinces of Holland were known as The Dutch Republic, they were not nearly republican enough for the revolutionary French. Apart from anything else, when electing their head of state – their Stadholder – the Dutch had got into the habit of electing the senior prince of the House of Orange, as though he was a hereditary monarch. So the French and their revolutionary Dutch allies were preparing a new constitution, and they were even planning to give the nation a new name: the Republic of Batavia.

All opposition had vanished. The Stadholder and his family had left for England. The British army was withdrawing across the north-eastern border. Recognising that its mission was now futile, the British naval squadron that had been waiting for the Princess had turned about and sailed for home. It was time to take the long route. But the winter was unusually hard. Some roads were impassable. Rivers were frozen. The northern German ports were inaccessible. Malmesbury took Princess Caroline back to Hanover, and for the next six weeks, in the exemplary decorum of the Hanoverian court, he continued to teach her how the English expected a princess to behave.

※

At last, when the thaw came, they headed north, accompanied by Mrs Harcourt, the wife of the British commander, who had agreed to attend the Princess on the journey. On 28 March they boarded a frigate, HMS *Jupiter*, off Cuxhaven at the mouth of the river Elbe. They were safe. Britannia still ruled the waves. The waters around them were crowded with British warships. A few days earlier, twenty miles to the south, the British expeditionary force had been evacuated from Bremerhaven.

When they reached Gravesend Malmesbury, Mrs Harcourt and Princess Caroline transferred from HMS *Jupiter* to the royal yacht, *Augusta*, and sailed up the Thames in her. They arrived at Greenwich, as expected, at noon on Easter Sunday.

The Princess stepped ashore eager and radiant. The limitations of a long sea voyage had given her ample excuse for not washing but, with the excited assistance of Mrs Harcourt, she had dressed more neatly than she had ever dressed before. She wore a muslin gown, a blue satin petticoat and a little black beaver hat with blue and black feathers in the hatband.

But there was no one there to meet her. The campaign to destroy her self-confidence had already begun.

The Prince of Wales had done his best. He had ordered carriages to be sent and had provided them with an escort from his own regiment, the 10th Light Dragoons, commanded by his two favourite officers, Lieutenant the Marquess of Worcester and Lieutenant George 'Beau' Brummell. But it was a matter of protocol that the royal bride's lady-in-waiting should go out in one of the carriages to greet her and escort her back into London, and the lady-in-waiting had delayed their departure.

It was over an hour before the carriages arrived and, when they did, rather than apologise, Lady Jersey greeted the Princess with patronising disapproval of her clothes. She was so rude that Malmesbury saw fit to step in and rebuke her for it. But Lady Jersey would not be put off. Although Princess Caroline's clothes were utterly appropriate for travelling in a carriage, Lady Jersey insisted that she should already be dressed as though she were about to be presented at court, and she forced the flustered Princess to change into a tight white satin dress and an unbecoming turban with tall ostrich feathers on it, both of which she just happened to have brought with her.

From Greenwich they drove through welcoming crowds to St James's Palace, where the Princess was to stay until her marriage. While she was acknowledging the cheers of the crowd at the open window, the Prince of Wales came into the room. Malmesbury, whom the Prince still addressed by his surname, described what happened next in the most famous passage of his diary:

> She very properly, in consequence of my saying to her it was the right mode of proceeding, attempted to kneel to him. He raised her (gracefully enough), and embraced her, said barely one word, turned round, retired to a distant part of the apartment, and calling me to him, said, 'Harris, I am not well; pray get me a glass of brandy.' I said, 'Sir, had you not better have a glass of water?' – upon which he, much out of humour, said with an oath, 'No; I will go directly to the Queen,' and away he went...

Princess Caroline gaped. 'My God!' she said, 'Is the Prince always like that?' And then, forgetting all that Malmesbury had taught her about tact and restraint, she added, 'I think he is very fat, and nothing like as handsome as his portrait.'

That evening they all dined together. By then the Prince had recovered his composure. But the Princess had not. She had clearly been hurt by her reception, and she dealt with her pain by being sarcastic, 'affecting raillery and wit, and throwing out coarse, vulgar hints...' making it plain that she was well aware of the relationship between her lady-in-waiting and her future husband. 'The Prince was disgusted', wrote Malmesbury, 'and this unfortunate dinner fixed his dislike'.

But there was no going back. Three days later Princess Caroline waited for her groom at the altar of the Chapel Royal, swaying precariously in an enormous, old-fashioned wedding dress with huge hoops inside it and broad ribbons with preposterously big bows wrapped around the outside – it had been chosen for her by the Queen.

Earlier that morning, the Prince had sent one of his brothers, the Duke of Clarence, to tell Mrs Fitzherbert that she was the only woman he would ever love. By the time he reached the chapel, it was obvious to everyone that this time no one had kept him from his brandy. He tottered reluctantly up the aisle, supported in every sense of the word by the Dukes of Bedford and Roxburghe.

The day ended in a manner that might have been expected. According to the new Princess of Wales, her husband 'passed the greatest part of his bridal night under the grate, where he fell, and where I left him'.

※

Thereafter the relationship continued as it had begun. For all that the

Princess was amiable and eager to please, there was no denying that she was slovenly and she smelt. The Prince displayed his displeasure at every opportunity, and the hurt Princess hit back each time by exaggerating whatever she had done to displease him.

Within three weeks of their wedding they were no longer living together as man and wife. At night the Princess retired to her own small apartments on the ground floor of Carlton House, and the Prince went to his much more splendid apartments above them.

Then came the development that really did fix the Prince's dislike for ever. He had married for money, and now he learned that, far from increasing his disposable income, his marriage had actually diminished it.

Pitt went further than he had promised. He persuaded Parliament to raise the allowance from the privy purse to as much as £125,000 a year. But the House of Commons also ruled that for the next nine years £65,000 of this, together with all the income from the Duchy of Cornwall, was to be set aside to pay off the Prince's debts. In real terms therefore his annual income had been reduced from £73,000 to £60,000; on top of that he now had the added expense of paying for his wife's establishment.

The Prince's distaste was embittered by resentment. He ignored his wife as much as he could by day as well as by night. On the pretext that he could no longer afford to pay for them, he removed most of the chairs from her private dining room and took back the pearl bracelets that he had given her on their wedding day – although he then gave them to Lady Jersey, who wore them publicly in her presence.

His displays of displeasure became increasingly cruel, and the Princess no longer felt strong enough to meet them all with defiance. Sometimes they reduced her to tears. As one witness, Lady Sheffield, wrote, she lost her 'lively spirits', and in their place her mood became one of 'melancholy and anxiety'.

As the months went by, however, it became clear that, somehow, during his first few days with his wife, the Prince had performed his dynastic duty. One day short of nine months after their wedding, she gave birth to Princess Charlotte.

The birth of a daughter did nothing to heal the royal relationship. At first the best that could be said was that the family was living under the same roof, the Prince and the Princess in their separate apartments and their daughter above them in the nursery. But when Charlotte was only just a year old, her miserable mother moved out and went to live in a villa five miles away near Blackheath.

The Princess of Wales still used her apartments in Carlton House when she came in to London to visit her daughter, and after a while Charlotte was sometimes taken out to visit her in Blackheath, although she was never allowed to stay with her.

During the first few years of her life, Charlotte saw more of her father than of her mother. But it was only just more. The Prince was often away from Carlton House, and when he was there his time with his daughter was always brief. Although he was said to be good with children, he only played with them and he soon tired of it. He devoted much more of his energy to preventing his wife and parents from influencing his daughter than he did to trying to influence her himself.

Eventually, however, when the Prince's affections were restored from Lady Jersey to Mrs Fitzherbert, he decided that he wanted Carlton House to himself again. So his wife was given apartments in Kensington Palace, and his eight-year-old daughter and all her staff were moved into Warwick House, a crumbling old brick building which stood just to the east of Carlton House.

From then on, for the rest of her childhood and throughout her youth, Princess Charlotte Augusta, who was fully expected to succeed her father one day as Queen of England, lived in a household of her own, in the company of no one who was not paid to be there.

Chapter Two

Warwick House

———

THE MOVE TO Warwick House was made all the more traumatic for Princess Charlotte by the fact that she had only recently acquired a completely new staff of governesses and senior tutors.

Indeed, there were only two members of her entire household who had been with her for any length of time at Carlton House. One was her personal maid, worthy Mrs Louis, the German widow of a British soldier. The other was her dresser, pretty Mrs Gagarin, who had innocently contracted a bigamous marriage with a Russian aristocrat and had kept his name, although not his title, when she left him soon after. Inevitably, in the circumstances, the little Princess was on what some saw as inappropriately intimate terms with these two, and their mutual devotion was to continue for the rest of their lives.

Charlotte's governess, Lady Elgin, had been asked to resign just before the move. Her only known offence had been to take Charlotte to visit her grandfather, the interfering old King. But she had done so without first obtaining permission from her father, and that had been more than enough to infuriate him.

When she went, the sub-governess, Miss Hayman, was dismissed as well. Miss Hayman's sin had been much more severe. She had become too friendly with Charlotte's mother. But the Princess of Wales stayed loyal to her. On her dismissal Miss Hayman joined the Princess's household in Blackheath and took charge of her privy purse.

In place of Lady Elgin, Charlotte's father appointed the Dowager Lady de Clifford, a dignified but barely graceful Irish woman, who was well past fifty years old. She had lived for some time at the Palace of Versailles before the French Revolution; and the Prince, who, despite his many faults, was justifiably renowned for his deportment, hoped in vain that she might be able to imbue his daughter with some of the qualities of that most elegant of courts.

Charlotte was a temperamental tomboy, and Lady de Clifford was too good natured to discipline her effectively. Every time she tried to be strict, the Princess was more than a match for her. Charlotte might not have wanted to behave like a princess, but she was all too well aware that she was one, and she used the fact whenever it suited her.

On one occasion, when she burst merrily into a room, Lady de Clifford attempted to scold. 'My dear Princess', she said, 'that is not civil; you should always shut the door after you when you come into a room'.

'Not I indeed', said Charlotte. 'If you want the door shut, ring the bell.'

Neither took their battles to heart, however. The antagonists were soon fond of each other, and Lady de Clifford did everything she could to make Charlotte's life less lonely.

At Carlton House, Charlotte's only playmate had been Annie Barnard, the orphaned niece of her father's coachman. Annie lived with her uncle and his wife above the stables and played with the Princess every day. She even dined with her, and for a few months they did their lessons together. But the move to Warwick House, beyond the safety of the stable-yard gates, was enough to separate them.

As a replacement for Annie, Lady de Clifford introduced the Princess to one of her grandsons, the Hon. George Keppel, who was three years younger than she was. George was a pupil nearby at Westminster School. He was brought round regularly in a coach to play with Charlotte at Warwick House – and to supplement his meagre school diet in the kitchens – and sometimes, appropriately chaperoned, she went round to visit him at the school.

Over forty years later, after he had succeeded his brother as Earl of Albemarle, George wrote a memoir which contains many of the most endearing anecdotes about the childhood of the Princess with 'blue eyes', 'peculiarly blond hair' and 'beautifully shaped' hands and feet. Among all the usual stories about fisticuffs, bolting horses and tears, he described an afternoon when Charlotte, who was visiting his parents' house in Earl's Court, crept out through a side gate and joined in at the back of a crowd that had assembled outside the main gate in the hope of catching a glimpse of the Princess.

He also recorded an afternoon when he and Charlotte helped out in the kitchen at Warwick House. As a result of their efforts, Lady de Clifford was served a mutton chop that was so heavily dressed and over-peppered that she summoned the servants in a fury. But he did not record whether the incident was an intentional prank or merely the result of childish over-enthusiasm.

Although Lady de Clifford dined at Warwick House, she did not live there. She came in from her own house every morning to supervise everything that went on. But she was not in overall command of Princess Charlotte's education. That was a responsibility for a man, a preceptor; at the instigation of the King, the office had been given to the Rt Rev. Dr John Fisher, Bishop of Exeter. Fisher was a favourite at Windsor Castle. He had been tutor to the Duke of Kent, Chaplain to the King, Clerk of the Closet and Canon of Windsor. He was sincerely pious and a connoisseur of painting and drawing.

But he was pompous, humourless, dogmatic, wilful and absurdly old-fashioned. In the manner of a generation that had mostly died out towards the end of the eighteenth century, he still wore a wig and spoke affectedly. When referring to himself, which he did often, he pronounced the word bishop 'bishup', emphasising the last syllable. Within weeks of meeting him, nine-year-old Charlotte had nicknamed him 'the Great UP'.

Lady de Clifford and the Prince of Wales were convinced that the King had appointed the Bishop to act as a spy and report back on everything that was happening at Warwick House. Delegating the duties of his distant diocese to his archdeacon, he called there regularly, sometimes as often as twice a week, and when he did he was almost always critical.

He argued constantly with Lady de Clifford about what Charlotte should be learning and how it should be taught to her. Their debates were heated, acrimonious and noisy, even in the presence of the Princess. But when that happened, Charlotte used to mock the Bishop behind his back, burdening Lady de Clifford with the added strain of trying to keep a straight face.

According to George Keppel, Charlotte had inherited her father's talents for acting and mimicry. While the Bishop pontificated, she stood behind him jutting out her lower lip, waving her arms and generally ridiculing his expressions and mannerisms in an exaggerated mime.

Deep down, Charlotte may have been disturbed by the extent to which Dr Fisher and Lady de Clifford argued, but the person who bore the brunt of the conflict was the Rev. Dr George Nott, her chaplain and sub-preceptor. Kindly, liberal, patient Dr Nott was responsible for religious instruction, English, Latin and ancient history, and he received conflicting instructions from the governess and preceptor in almost every field. On top of that, since he saw himself as Charlotte's moral tutor, he added to his burden by trying to teach her to be honest. But he was no more successful in that than in spelling.

Charlotte wanted to mend her ways. She liked Dr Nott and was eager to please him. She told him so several times. In one note to him she wrote, 'Let me most humbly implore your forgiveness... Never shall another lie come out of me.' But, like many children in discordant households, she had discovered that a little falsehood here and there could go a long way towards establishing her innocence or reducing the burden of her studies; it was a tool too useful to abandon completely.

Apart from Dr Nott, there were two other sub-preceptors, who came in as he did to teach English literature, French, German and modern history; and there were masters for music, dancing, drawing and writing. The only resident members of Charlotte's tutorial staff were the two widows who acted as sub-governesses, Mrs Campbell, whose husband had been a Governor of Bermuda, and Mrs Udney, whose husband, according to the Prince of Wales, had been the ugliest man he ever saw.

Mrs Campbell was small, angular and argumentative. Unknown to the Prince of Wales, who affected support for the Whig opposition, she was also, like Dr Fisher, a high Tory. But she was intelligent and strong-willed. As a governess she was strict but fair, and Charlotte respected her for it. Before long the Princess was announcing poignantly that Mrs Campbell and Dr Nott were her adopted parents.

Mrs Udney, on the other hand, was good-looking, ill-tempered and fickle. She was so fond of drink that even Charlotte noticed, and she adored gossip. According to Lord Glenbervie, who heard it from Mrs (by then Lady) Harcourt, she took one of Charlotte's tutors as a lover. Sadly, however, he was unable to name him. In a letter to his wife, who was one of Lady Jersey's successors as lady-in-waiting to Charlotte's mother, he wrote, 'She says Mrs Udney had an intrigue with one of the Princess Charlotte's music or drawing masters – that they used to be locked up together in Mrs Udney's room, which opened into the Princess's, and that when any friend or intimate came there, and was going to open the door of communication, the Princess would say: "You must not try to go there. Mrs Udney and —— are there, and they always lock themselves in."'

Although Mrs Udney tried to worm her way into Charlotte's affections by indulging her, she was never successful. The Princess, who referred to her behind her back as 'Mrs Nibs', was unimpressed by her fondness for drink and her depravity, and she may have had other unrecorded reasons for disliking her as well. But to Lady de Clifford and Dr Nott, Mrs Udney's most serious weakness was her fondness for gossip. The drawing rooms of London were buzzing with scandalous stories about Charlotte's parents, particularly her mother, and there was a real danger that sooner or later Mrs Udney might pass some of them on to her.

In his pursuit of pleasure, the Prince of Wales often went away from London for weeks or even months on end, and when he was away it was not thought to be seemly for Charlotte and her household to be left unsupervised. When he was in residence at Carlton House, his visits to his daughter next door were never frequent and always brief, but at least he could say that he was on hand and that Charlotte was nominally under his protection. So when he went away – to Brighton or Newmarket or to stay with friends – Charlotte and her household, including Lady de Clifford, moved to Windsor, where she could be under the nominal protection of the King. But they did not live in the castle. As in London, they lived separately in their own house, Lower Lodge, in the park.

❋

In March 1806, while they were living at Windsor, ten-year-old Charlotte went into a room where Mrs Campbell was writing at a table. When Charlotte asked what she was doing, Mrs Campbell answered that she was making her will.

'Then I'll make mine too', said Charlotte. And so she did, in the same childish detail as she kept her accounts.

I make my will. First I leave all my best books, and all my books, to the Rev. Mr. Nott.

Secondly, to Mrs. Campbell my three watches and half my jewels.

Thirdly, I beg Mr. Nott, whatever money he finds me in possession of, to distribute to the poor, and all my money I leave to the poor to them. I leave with Mr. Nott all my papers which he knows of, and I beg him to burn those which he sealed up. I beg the Prayer Book which Lady Elgin gave me may be given to the Bishop of Exeter, and the Bible Lady Elgin gave me may be given to him also. Also all my playthings the Miss Fishers are to have. And lastly, concerning Mrs. Gagarin and Mrs. Louis, I beg that they may be very handsomly paid, and that they may have a house. Lady de Clifford the rest of my jewels, except those that are most valuable, and those I beg my father and mother, the Prince and Princess of Wales, to take. Nothing to Mrs. Udney, for reasons. I have done my will, and trust that after I am dead a great deal may be done for Mr. Nott. I hope the King will make him a Bishop.

Charlotte.

March, 1806.

My birds to Mrs. Gagarin and my dog or dogs to Mrs. Anna Hatton my chambermaid.

When Dr Nott saw the will, he entered into the spirit of the game and suggested that Charlotte was being too unkind to Mrs Udney. Charlotte agreed and added a codicil making a bequest to Mrs Udney as well. But by then, somehow – and it is not difficult to guess how – the original will had found its way into the hands of the Prince of Wales, who allowed himself to be convinced that it had been written under the influence of Mrs Campbell.

Before making any decision, however, he consulted the Privy

Council. The spring of 1806 stood at the centre of a great crisis in the history of Europe. Less than six months before the little will was written, Britain's hero, Admiral Lord Nelson, had died saving his nation from invasion at the battle of Trafalgar. The French army that had been waiting to be carried across the Channel had turned east. Just over a month later the armies of Britain's allies Austria and Russia had been shattered at Austerlitz. Napoleon was the master of most of Europe. At his instigation, King George's Electorate of Hanover had been given to the Prussians. And on top of all that, Britain's brilliant Prime Minister, William Pitt, had died heart-broken and exhausted. The coalition that replaced him, known optimistically as 'the ministry of all the talents', was negotiating for peace with Napoleon.

Yet at that most desperate moment, some of the men who had been entrusted with the safety of the nation were asked to devote time to discussing the implications of a will written on impulse by a lonely ten-year-old child.

To anyone who knew the truth, their judgement cannot have been encouraging. They agreed that Mrs Campbell was responsible.

Mrs Campbell was asked to resign, and Dr Nott, overwhelmed with remorse and frustration, took to his bed and stayed there for several weeks. Charlotte was told only that Mrs Campbell had resigned on grounds of ill health. She wrote in her misery to George's mother, Lady Albemarle:

> Poor dear Mrs. Campbell is going away, for her health is so bad. If you have any regard to me, you will write to her and try to console her. Do if you love me. I lose a great deal when she leaves me. Indeed she is a charming woman, that is far above Mrs. Udney, for the more I see of Mrs. Campbell, the more I love [her], but Mrs. Udney I still continue to dislike. When you come to town I wish to have a conversation with you about her... You have no idea how unhappy I am.

CHAPTER THREE

'The Delicate Investigation'

H IS DAUGHTER'S WILL was not the only family business with which the Prince of Wales burdened his father's ministers in the spring of 1806.

Like everyone in London society, the Prince had heard scores of lurid stories about the life his wife was leading in Blackheath. It was said that her dinner parties often ended in unseemly games of blind man's buff, that she was in the habit of leaving the room with gentlemen guests and not returning for more than an hour, that she had given birth to a child and that she had had dozens of lovers, among them the treasurer of the navy, George Canning, two naval officers, the dashing Captain Sir Sidney Smith and Captain Thomas Manby, and the painter Sir Thomas Lawrence, who was known to have slept in her house while painting her portrait.

If the Prince could prove the worst of these stories, there was a chance that he might be allowed to bring an action for divorce against his wife; towards the end of 1805 he was approached by a Lieutenant-Colonel of marines, Sir John Douglas, with what looked like all the proof he needed.

For a few years Sir John and Lady Douglas had been the closest of friends with the Princess of Wales. But she had then rejected them so completely and cruelly that they were determined to have their revenge. They were now prepared to reveal everything they knew, or claimed to know, about her, and in the course of several long sessions with the Prince and his advisers, they told it all in great detail.

All the stories of lovers were true, they said. The Princess was insatiable. She had even embarrassed the beautiful but vulgar Lady Douglas by regularly making intimate advances to her. Worst of all, they claimed, they could confirm that she had indeed given birth to a child.

Among the seven or eight poor children whom the eccentric Princess had adopted informally and then farmed out to live with friends, there was one favourite, William Austin, whom she kept in her own household. According to the Douglases, the Princess had told them that the boy was her own son. Furthermore she had told both them and others that the father was none other than the Prince of Wales. The child had been conceived, she said, during an attempted reconciliation on her last visit to Carlton House.

If the last part of that story had been true, it would have had devastating implications. It would have meant that little 'Willikin' and not Charlotte was second in line to the throne of England. But the Prince of Wales knew better than anyone that it was not true, although, to his delight, he could not be so sure about the rest of the story, or indeed about any of the others.

The Prince took the Douglases' 'written declarations' to the Lord Chancellor, who felt that in the light of the last allegations there had to be some sort of enquiry. So the Lord Chancellor went to the Prime Minister, and then, to the further delight of the Prince, the Prime Minister went to the King.

At first King George was reluctant to do anything. He was fond of the Princess of Wales. Despite her estrangement from his son, he still visited her often at Blackheath. But eventually he was persuaded and gave orders for what became known as 'The Delicate Investigation'.

❋

On 31 May, the Prime Minister, the Home Secretary, the Lord Chancellor, the Lord Chief Justice and the Solicitor General assembled at Number 10 Downing Street. In the course of that session and the many that followed, they examined the Douglases, several doctors, all the servants who now worked for the Princess and most of those who had ever worked for her.

Their evidence was not as helpful as the Prince had hoped, however. They could not corroborate the story that his wife was the mother of William Austin. Apart from anything else, there was a Mrs Austin who called herself his mother and came over regularly from Deptford to visit him. Indeed none of the servants could say for certain that the Princess had ever given birth to a child at Blackheath, and when asked if they thought she had ever looked pregnant, a few said yes, some said no and some said she was so fat that it was impossible to tell.

As for the men named in the rumours and the 'written declarations', there was no hard evidence that any of them had actually committed treasonable adultery with the Princess. George Canning was just one of her many visitors. Although she had been seen kissing Captain Manby and sitting very close to Sir Sidney on a sofa, no one had caught her with either of them in any more compromising circumstances. Although Sir Thomas had twice stayed at the house, he had remained in his room all night.

Nevertheless, it seemed likely from all that was said that the Princess had had plenty of lovers. Several more names were suggested, and several were left un-named. As with the captains and the portrait painter, there was not enough evidence to prove beyond doubt that any of them was guilty, but that of course did not mean that any or all of them were innocent.

Although the servants could not confirm any specific allegation, they succeeded in convincing the committee that their mistress's life was neither celibate nor seemly. The tone of their testimony was summed up simply in the words of the handsomest young footman, Samuel Roberts. 'The Princess', he said, 'is very fond of fucking'.

The committee, which had not allowed the Princess of Wales or any of her alleged lovers to cross-examine the witnesses, submitted its report to the King on 14 July. It had concluded that there was 'no foundation for believing' that the Princess of Wales had borne any child since moving to Blackheath, but it felt strongly that there were 'other particulars respecting the conduct of her Royal Highness, such as must, especially considering her exalted rank and station, necessarily give occasion to very unfavourable interpretations'.

The Prince of Wales was bitterly disappointed. His father's ministers had let him down. Their disapproval was not enough. They had found him no grounds for divorce.

His wife, on the other hand, was self-righteously triumphant. During the 'Delicate Investigation' the King had not visited her, and he had not invited her to visit him. But now that she had been acquitted by his arbitrary tribunal, she felt that it was his duty to acknowledge her innocence publicly by inviting her to court again. She wrote to the King asking him to receive her, but the King was not so sure that he should. There was much in the report that could not be condoned. So the Princess of Wales decided to write to him again. Since she had not been allowed to present her defence to the committee in Downing Street, she would present it to the King in Windsor instead.

With the best but biased legal advice from Spencer Perceval, who had recently resigned the office of Attorney General after the death of Pitt, she laid out her detailed rebuttal of every charge that the Douglases had brought against her. Her letter, dated 2 October, was so long that it became known sarcastically as 'The Book'.

Nine weeks later, when she had received no reply, not even an acknowledgement, the Princess wrote to the King again begging him to receive her and restore her reputation. At the same time, however, in a barely veiled threat, she arranged to have copies of 'The Book' printed.

Nevertheless, it was another seven weeks before the Lord Chancellor's office informed the Princess that, despite his reservations, the King was now ready to receive her. But week after week went by without any invitation arriving. Eventually, on 5 March 1807, five months after her first letter, the Princess of Wales lifted the veil from her threat. If she did not receive an invitation within the next week, she would publish 'The Book'.

By then the gossips in London society had exhausted their imaginations speculating about what 'The Delicate Investigation' had discovered and about what might be in 'The Book'. To the press and the general public, who knew very little about the Princess of Wales and a great deal that they did not like about her husband, she was a wronged woman who deserved their support. The reputation of the royal family sank even further.

Spencer Perceval believed, and indeed hoped, that publication of 'The Book' would bring down the government that had treated the Princess so shoddily. But, as it turned out, there was never any need for publication. A few days later, the coalition government destroyed itself. The Cabinet resigned, bitterly divided over whether or not Roman Catholics should be allowed to sit in Parliament and hold commissions in the army.

The Tories were returned to office. George Canning became Foreign Secretary and Spencer Perceval became Chancellor of the Exchequer. The Princess of Wales had friends in high places.

❋

While Perceval bought back the copies of 'The Book' that he knew had already been distributed, Canning persuaded the Prime Minister, the Duke of Portland, to speak to the King. On 18 May, almost a year after the first session of 'The Delicate Investigation', the Princess of Wales was again received at court.

Throughout the investigation and the stand-off that followed, Charlotte continued to visit her mother, although Willikin was no longer allowed to be present and, as always, the Princess was accompanied, usually by Lady de Clifford. When the two went out to Blackheath on 14 July 1807, after her mother had been restored to royal favour, Charlotte was introduced to her maternal grandmother, the old Duchess of Brunswick. On land at least, Napoleon was still marching from success to success. In the previous year the King of Prussia had been persuaded to declare war on him again, and on 14 October the Prussian armies had been routed by the French at Jena and Auerstadt. The old Duke of Brunswick, again in command, had been mortally wounded in the eye. Since then Napoleon had overrun Brunswick and incorporated it into his Confederation of the Rhine. The Duchess was a widow and a stateless fugitive.

She was also a renowned gossip, but, as on previous visits, the presence of Lady de Clifford prevented anyone from mentioning the investigation or 'The Book' in front of Charlotte. As Lady de Clifford and Dr Nott knew well, the only real danger that someone might do that lay with the ingratiating Mrs Udney. Whether she did or not, however, Mrs Udney must have known that they thought she might, and it seems that she decided to divide her enemies and undermine the weakest of them.

In December 1807 someone gave the Prince of Wales a note which Dr Nott had written to Princess Charlotte rebuking her for not turning up for a lesson. There is no direct evidence that the culprit was Mrs Udney, but she was the only member of Charlotte's household who had the opportunity, a motive and access to the Prince. The Prince wrote to Dr Fisher. In his opinion 'a remonstrance on the failure might have been made in terms of becoming deference'. But Mr Nott, as he called him, was overreaching his authority in presuming to criticise the Princess. 'Mr Nott is paid to wait for the

Princess, instead of being entitled to expect that she should wait for him.'

The Bishop defended Dr Nott valiantly, reminding the Prince that he was a man of many virtues and an example to his daughter, and for the time being the Prince was placated. Just over a year later, however, Mrs Udney discovered that Lady de Clifford and Dr Nott were about to have her disciplined. They had learned, perhaps from Charlotte, that she had shown the Princess an obscene cartoon of Nelson's mistress, Lady Hamilton, and had explained the meaning to her. They had already reported the matter to the Bishop, and the Bishop had consulted the Lord Chancellor.

Mrs Udney decided to strike first. She went to the Prince of Wales and complained about Dr Nott. He was always gossiping with Princess Charlotte in order to exercise undue influence and he encouraged her to be disrespectful about Lady de Clifford and even her father.

The Prince of Wales was already prejudiced against Dr Nott, partly because of the earlier impertinence and partly because he suspected that the sub-preceptor had prevented him from seeing some papers in which his daughter had been disparaging about her mother. He believed Mrs Udney's preposterous story.

This time the Bishop pleaded in vain. Dr Nott was suspended from office and never reinstated, and the Bishop and Lady de Clifford decided that this was not the moment to take the case against Mrs Udney any further.

Charlotte wrote to Dr Nott. 'If we never meet again, keep for me your regard and affection. If I go into other people's hands, rely on me, I shall ever remember your kindness and your good advice.'

The year 1809 had deprived thirteen-year-old Charlotte of her second 'adopted parent'. But it also brought her two new friends. The first was a real relation, her uncle William, the new Duke of Brunswick. The bluff but dignified and patient Duke was relieved to have reached London safely, and he never seemed to tire of listening to Charlotte's lisping chatter.

After the duchy had been overrun, he had assembled seven hundred exiled hussars and dressed them in black uniforms in permanent mourning for his father. With this resolute little corps, he had reconquered the duchy. But the French had returned in strength and driven him out again. Dodging the French whenever he could and fighting them when he had no choice, he had led his men westward to the coast, where a squadron of British warships was waiting to carry them to England. In the years to come the romantic Black Brunswickers were to be among Britain's most formidable allies in the war against Napoleon.

Like many military men in Europe, and like very few in clean-shaven England, the Duke had a huge moustache. Charlotte adored it. After their first meeting in Blackheath, according to George Keppel, she went back to Warwick House, painted a black moustache on her face and marched up and down in a military manner barking guttural expletives, which she hoped very much sounded like German swear words.

The other friend was introduced to Charlotte by Dr Nott's replacement, the Rev. Dr William Short. Dr Short was handsome and a bit more of a dandy than most clergymen. He was always light-hearted, even though he had recently been widowed and was still receiving consoling letters and visits from members of his wife's family.

One of these was his brother-in-law, a distinguished admiral, who had been raised to the peerage as Baron Keith of Stonehaven Marischal. Lord Keith's first wife, a Scots heiress, had died shortly after giving birth to their daughter, and that girl, now twenty-one years old, self-confident and strikingly beautiful, had inherited her mother's enormous fortune. She was the embodiment of Jane Austen's Emma – 'handsome, clever and rich'. Charlotte worshipped her the moment she met her. Here at last was the companion, confidante and counsellor that the Princess had always needed. Her name was the Hon. Margaret Mercer Elphinstone.

Chapter Four

First Love

————

Princess Charlotte wrote frequently to her 'dearest Miss Mercer', and Mercer Elphinstone kept almost all the letters. In later life she resisted every demand to hand them over. The best that she was prepared to do was to destroy those that were 'upon particular subjects'.

Whether she did or not can never be known. Before she died, however, she gave all the letters that were still in her possession to her daughter, who married the fourth Marquess of Lansdowne, and they remained in his family until sold in 1994. Due to Mercer's defiance, they were never read by the contemporary royal family. But they have survived to be read by posterity, and they are a moving testament to the hopes and fears of the ill-fated Princess.

The earliest letters are little more than gushing expressions of affection and eagerness for news. On the whole, the most amusing passages are the regular disparaging references to Mrs Udney. Yet even in these letters there is a sense of threat and caution. The fifteen-year-old Princess had already endured enough to know that, if she was going to be frank, she would also have to be careful.

One of the first letters begins, 'I must scrawl you a few lines tonight otherwise I have no chance of writing in the daytime without being looked over, &c.

'We arrived at Windsor Castle just as 4 struck & was very graciously recvd. by the Queen & very kindly by the Princesses. Heavens how dul...'

When that letter was written, at the beginning of June 1811, the atmosphere in Windsor Castle was more likely to have been bitter than dull. The King's latest bout of insanity had lasted so long that no one now expected him to recover. In January the government had brought in the Regency Bill. On 6 February, while Charlotte rode up and down in the garden, peering through the windows of Carlton House to see what was going on, the Prince of Wales had been formally sworn in as Prince Regent. Charlotte's father was now nominal head of state, and her grandmother and most of her aunts and uncles were more inclined to feel gloomy than glad about it.

Typically, the Prince Regent decided to celebrate his appointment with an extravagant fête at Carlton House. His excuse was to entertain the exiled pretender to the throne of France, Louis-Philippe, who had actually been living in Twickenham for the last ten years. But the real reason was to mark the opening of what he hoped would be his own splendid reign.

When she heard about it, Charlotte felt sure that she would be invited, that her first ball would be this memorable event. But there was never any chance of that. As Lady Rose Weigall put it:

The Regent had reason to fear that her appearance in public would give a fresh stimulus to the widespread feeling in favour of herself and her mother and render him proportionately more unpopular. He was further bent upon avoiding everything which could look like a recognition of her as the heir presumptive to the Crown, probably hoping that by the death of his wife or by a divorce he might hereafter have a son through a second marriage and shut out the

daughter of his deserted consort from the throne... For these reasons
the Princess Charlotte was regarded as a rival to be suppressed rather
than as a future sovereign.

And that was why Charlotte was writing to Mercer from Windsor.
Her father wanted her out of the way.

A few days earlier, when she still half-hoped for an invitation,
Charlotte had written to one of her former sub-governesses, Miss
Hayman, who was now on her mother's staff in Blackheath, telling
her about the great event and describing an evening with her mother,
who was now spending more and more of her time in her apartments
in Kensington Palace.

> My Dear Hamy, But a few lines, as I will write you a longer one soon
> again, only to tell you that the Prince Regent gives a magnificent
> ball on the 5th of June. I have not been invited, nor do I know if
> I shall be or not. If I should not, it will make a great noise in the
> world, as the friends I have seen have repeated over and over again
> it is my duty to go there; it is proper that I should. Really I do think
> it will be very hard if I am not asked. The Duke of Gloucester dined
> on the 16th at Kensington Palace, and was as usual delightful; he
> was very kind to me and talked a great part of the evening to me on
> the sofa alone; his charming sister was also there, who was as kind to
> me as possible. In short, there is hardly a moment of my life that I
> passed so happily as I did the other night. The 17th the Princess was
> perfectly out of humour and quite snappish; what had happened
> God only knows.

At this stage in her life Charlotte was clearly much more aware of her
political position as a Princess than she was of her feminine charm
or even her eligibility. The reason why the Duke of Gloucester had
been 'delightful' on so many occasions was quite simply because he
was attracted to her.

Her father was already aware of it, and was not pleased. His cousin the Duke was entirely unsuitable for Charlotte. Apart from anything else he was more than twenty years older than she was, and had also been paying court for years to the Regent's sister Princess Mary.

The charms that delighted the Duke of Gloucester did not, however, have much chance to delight any other gentleman during the early summer. The great fête came and went. For a few days afterwards Carlton House was opened to the public, so that everyone could see the magnificent decorations. But Princess Charlotte remained in Windsor at Lower Lodge, writing regularly in good humoured desperation to ask Mercer for 'a little London news'.

Lady Albinia Campbell, who visited Windsor during June, wrote to her daughter describing the Princess:

> She is grown and improved in looks, but I do not think her manner dignified, as a Princess's ought to be, or, indeed, as I should wish a daughter of mine to behave. She hates her 'Granny', as she calls her – loves nobody except Princesses Mary and Sophia, goes swaggering about, and she twangs hands with all the men, is in awe of no one and glories in her independent way of thinking. Her passion is horses – that and mathematics are the only amusements she has. Her riding is beautiful – no fear of course – gallops and leaps over every ditch like a schoolboy – gave her groom a cut with her whip about the back to-day and told him he was always in the way. This was in good humour though, but it is not acting en Princesse.

In July, with relief, Charlotte returned to Warwick House and renewed her regular but now less frequent visits to her mother at Kensington Palace. Lady Glenbervie, who was present at one of these, seems to have shared the reservations of Lady Albinia. She admitted that Charlotte was 'grown tall and very graceful', but she added that she was 'forward, dogmatic on all subjects, buckish about horses, and full of exclamations very like swearing.'

Like most young ladies in those days, Charlotte wore long drawers, and when she stretched out in a chair after dinner they showed beyond the hem of her dress.

Lady de Clifford suggested that she should adopt a more dignified position. 'My dear Princess Charlotte', she said, 'You show your drawers.'

'I never do but where I can put myself at my ease', said Charlotte.

'Yes, my dear', said Lady de Clifford, presuming to contradict her, 'When you get out of your carriage.'

'I don't care if I do', said Charlotte.

Lady de Clifford pressed her point. 'Your drawers are much too long', she said.

'I do not think so', said the Princess. 'The Duchess of Bedford's are much longer, and they are bordered with Brussels lace.'

'Oh', said Lady de Clifford, giving in as always. 'If she is to wear them she does well to make them handsome.'

✵

That evening in Kensington Palace may have been the last outing of Princess Charlotte the total tomboy. A few days earlier, on 11 October, she had written to Mercer, 'George FitzClarence is arrived from Portugal; I saw him the very day he arrived in town, much grown & looking very well. At present he is in town but joins the Prince's regiment at Brighton soon. He told me the troops were in good spirits, but that the French were 20 thousand <u>stronger</u> than us.'

Tall, dark and handsome Captain George FitzClarence was Charlotte's illegitimate cousin. His father was her uncle William, Duke of Clarence – the future King William IV. His mother was Mrs Jordan, the most popular and admired actress on the London stage. Two years older than Charlotte, he was an officer in her father's regiment, the 10th, which was now designated hussars and dressed even more extravagantly than before.

But George's commission was no sinecure. He had seen action and had already demonstrated the qualities that would one day earn him the earldom of Munster and the exalted rank of Major-General. At the age of only fifteen he had joined the little British army in Portugal. Since then, commanded by Arthur Wellesley, who had been rewarded for his success with the title of Viscount Wellington, that army had chased the French back into Spain and was now advancing after them; George had served with it all the way. Only five months before his regiment returned to England, he had been captured by the French while lying wounded on the battlefield of Fuentes de Onoro, and had escaped a few days later when his wounds were only half healed.

George was on leave, and he was so taken with his royal cousin that he went out as often as he could to ride beside her carriage when she took the air in the parks of London or Windsor.

In Windsor in particular, Lady de Clifford had always dreaded these daily excursions. The Princess often took the reins herself, and would frequently leave the track and drive hard at every bump in the ground, rejoicing in Lady de Clifford's discomfort as she bounced around in terror. But now there was a different cause for dread, even though it made Charlotte's conduct more sedate. In an age that judged so much by appearances, it was unseemly for a young lady to be seen chatting to the same officer beside her carriage day after day, just as it was unseemly for her to be seen sitting alone on a sofa with the same gentleman for any length of time.

Lady de Clifford felt that it was her duty to report the matter to the Prince Regent, although she assured him, justifiably, that the relationship was entirely innocent.

It should have been a relief to her therefore when, after only six weeks, George FitzClarence rejoined his regiment in Brighton. But by then she was obliged to report that there was another illegitimate cousin riding devotedly beside the carriage in his place.

This was Lieutenant Charles Hesse of the 18th King's Irish

Hussars. His father was the Duke of York, and his mother, it was said, was an aristocratic German lady. He was not nearly as tall as George FitzClarence and, like many officers in Irish regiments in those days, he was a little bit of a rogue, but, like almost all of them, he was engagingly charming. And Charlotte adored him.

There is no record of how Charlotte met her 'little lieutenant'. She may have been introduced to him by George FitzClarence, or she may have met him through her mother. Like all sensible suitors, Charles Hesse paid court to Charlotte's mother, to such an extent that she later told Mercer she was not sure whether he was her lover or her mother's. The Princess of Wales used Charles to carry letters to her daughter, which of course was a good excuse to ride up to her carriage, and Charlotte used her mother as one of the several couriers who carried her letters to Charles. For two or three months, between their meetings, she wrote to him recklessly and gave him presents, and she continued to write to him after he went down to Portsmouth to prepare for his regiment's embarkation for Spain.

Lady de Clifford was well aware that Charlotte and Charles were too fond of each other. She tried to prevent their meetings in the park, but as always she lost the argument. As a woman of the world – as a woman who had lived at the French court – she must also have been made suspicious by Charlotte's long absences during some of their visits to Kensington Palace. But she may not have known for certain, as others did, that the Princess of Wales had let Lieutenant Hesse into the palace through the garden door. During those absences, he and Princess Charlotte were locked up together in her mother's bedchamber.

Like the rest of the royal family, Charles's father, the Duke of York, was at least aware of the inappropriate meetings in the park. But he did not feel inclined to reproach anyone. He was one of the many who disapproved of the way in which the Prince Regent prevented his daughter from appearing in public or even in society. If the Princess was lonely, she could hardly be criticised for taking pleasure in such company as she could find. His Duchess agreed with him. So they decided that, if the Regent was not prepared to bring his daughter out, they would do it for him. They would invite Princess Charlotte to stay at Oatlands, their country house in Surrey, and while she was there they would give a ball.

✻

The childless Duchess of York, whose uncle was Frederick the Great, respected her husband as a soldier, but in most other ways she preferred the company of her menagerie to his. Nevertheless she knew her duty. She tolerated his infidelities with dignity. She turned his country house into a comfortable home. When he went there with his many crude companions, she had a warm welcome for all of them. She was a generous hostess. She served dinner much later than anyone else in England, and like her husband she was happy to sit up all night afterwards playing cards. She hated ceremony. At Oatlands there was none of the stiff formality that pervaded the households of the other royal dukes. In atmosphere it was more like a little German palace or the home of an English country gentleman. Everyone who went there spoke well of it. The only drawbacks, they said, were the smell and the insanitary condition of the carpets – very few of the Duchess's forty dogs were house-trained.

Charlotte went to Oatlands in November. The Duchess had laid on everything possible to make the stay enjoyable. Among the guests in the houseparty there were several of Charlotte's age, including Anne and Georgiana Fitzroy, the nieces of Lord Wellington. Expeditions were arranged almost every day. On one day they went to Hampton Court Palace, which Charlotte described to Mercer as having 'an air of gloom & coldness about it which is frightful'. On another they went to 'the famous house' at Paines Hill. And then they visited a house called Claremont.

They drove over to Claremont twice. On the first day they were shown round the elegant Palladian mansion, which Clive of India had begun to build over forty years earlier. On the second they inspected the splendid park, which had been designed by 'Capability' Brown. Clive had committed suicide before he could enjoy it, and since then there had been so many owners that no family had lived there long enough to make it a home.

Charlotte did not share her first impression of Claremont with Mercer. But another visitor, a few months later, gave hers. 'It is', wrote Jane Austen sadly and prophetically, 'a house that seems never to have prospered'.

The climax of the visit was not one ball but two. The first, according to Charlotte's letters, did not end until after 2 am, and on the on the following night the waltzing went on until after four. Charlotte 'enjoyed it of all things', despite the conduct of her father, who had grudgingly agreed to be among the many guests. On the first evening he hurt her, and shocked everyone else, by ignoring her. On the second, while the Scottish Member of Parliament William Adam was attempting to teach her the 'Highland Flurry', he insisted on joining in the demonstration.

For a moment or two the Regent and Mr Adam, who was Mercer's uncle, reeled round the room together. Then the Prince struck his shoe against the leg of a sofa, fell over and tore a tendon in his foot. Being the man he was, he made a fuss, retired to bed and remained at Oatlands for over a fortnight.

Inevitably, when the story got out, the Prince's many enemies said that he had obviously been drunk. But, if he had been, Charlotte would have admitted it to Mercer. According to her letters the only guest who got 'beastly drunk' was Richard Brinsley Sheridan, remembered now as a playwright but equally well known then as a leading member of the Whig opposition.

Having introduced the Princess to the waltz, clearly the Duchess of York's next duty was to take her to the opera. The visit was arranged to take place on 22 February the following year, when Charlotte would have passed her sixteenth birthday. Meanwhile the Duke attempted to improve her mind, and perhaps her English, by lending her an anonymous novel, which both he and she believed had been written by Lady Anne Paget.

Charlotte loved it and wrote to Mercer. '"Sence and Sencibility" I have <u>just finished</u> reading; it certainly is interesting, & you feel quite one of the company. I think Maryanne & me are very like <u>in disposition</u>, that certainly I am not so good, the same imprudence, &c, however remain very like.'

CHAPTER FIVE

The Radical Princess

———◦———

A s THE DAY for the visit to the opera approached, Charlotte also agreed to dine with her father on that evening. There was no conflict in this. It was customary in those days to dine before going to the opera or the theatre; the Prince Regent, like most people, dined in the late afternoon.

There were sixteen at the dinner, among them the Duke of York, but not the Duchess, and politicians from both parties, including Sheridan and Adam. As it was bound to do, the conversation turned to politics. When too much wine had been consumed, the Prince launched into a vehement attack on the Whigs. He censured the leader of the Whig opposition, Earl Grey, for not having joined a coalition in the previous year, when he was offered the opportunity, and he censured the Duke of York for corresponding with him about a possible future government.

Until he was sworn in as Regent, the Prince had been an ostentatious Whig himself. At one of his daughter's birthday parties he had told the guests proudly that he was having her educated to espouse the ideals of Charles James Fox. Once he became Regent, therefore, the Whigs fully expected that, after a year, when he would have the power to do so, he would dismiss the government and call a general election.

By now, however, it was clear to everyone that he was never going to do any such thing. After all, it was the Tory government, now led by Spencer Perceval, that had made him Regent, and it was the Tory government that was winning the war in Spain. It was neither in his interest nor the nation's to risk a general election at such a moment.

To Charlotte her father's conduct was nothing short of a betrayal. She was the Whig he once wanted her to be, despite the influence of Tory tutors. She could never be as fickle as he was. As a Whig she was sincere, committed and above all radical. Her letters to Mercer are full of recommendations of Whig pamphlets and journals. Shortly before the dinner she had written to her about what her father and his government were doing to suppress the Roman Catholic majority in Ireland. In a letter so passionate that her respect for grammar and syntax was even less evident than usual, she wrote:

I do <u>indeed</u> feel <u>very very</u> unhappy & uneasy about this business in Ireland; it but too too clearly shows the side he has taken. Good God, what will become of us! Of Ireland! We shall <u>without doubt</u> lose that, & as English people <u>all faith & confidence</u> in their Prince. Don't call me a <u>croker</u> after all this, nor a <u>republican</u> for saying that the Irish <u>will be justified</u> in anything they do, if their long promised freedom is not granted.

As the conversation at the dinner table became more and more heated, Charlotte became more and more agitated. The Duke of York defended himself. Lord Lauderdale defended Lord Grey, who was no longer welcome at Carlton House. Eventually Charlotte burst into tears, stood up and turned to leave. Sheridan, not yet too drunk not to be chivalrous, left his seat and escorted her to the door.

Back at Warwick House Charlotte composed herself enough to make the short journey to Covent Garden. As she and the Duchess of York entered their box at the opera house, she waved over-excitedly to everyone she knew in the stalls. A few judged her behaviour a little undignified, but to most people it was charming. Then she noticed that the box opposite was occupied by Earl Grey. Here was a chance to tell the world where her political loyalties lay. Having already attracted his attention, she leaned out and, for all to see, blew kisses at the leader of the opposition.

A few days later, after the Whig gossips had spread the story of the dinner party throughout London, 'dear Lord Byron', whom Charlotte had been 'seeing a great deal lately', wrote a short poem in praise of the Princess who did not yet know how popular she was. It was entitled 'To a Lady Weeping'.

> Weep, daughter of a noble line,
>   A sire's disgrace, a realm's decay —
> Ah! happy if each tear of thine
>   Could wash a father's fault away!
>
> Weep, for thy tears are virtue's tears,
>   Auspicious to these suffering isles —
> And be each drop, in future years,
>   Repaid thee of thy people's smiles.

❊

Over the next few months the Prince Regent stiffened his loyalty to the Tories. When Spencer Perceval was assassinated by a lunatic on 11 May, he did not call a general election. Instead he invited Lord Liverpool to form another Tory government. But at the same time he grew more and more paranoid about the influence the Whigs were having on his family. He knew that his wife was now being advised by Whigs, and he knew that Mercer Elphinstone was as radical as any of them. So he gave orders that Charlotte and her mother were to see each other as seldom as possible, that all Charlotte's letters were to be opened and read by his agents at the Post Office, and he told his daughter that she must no longer meet with Mercer or even write to her.

Charlotte managed to obey the last order for all of six months. But it was not an order she could obey for ever – and it was not one that she found difficult to disobey. She was already experienced and accomplished in the art of sending secret letters. The world was full of bribable grooms and sympathetic ladies-in-waiting. On 24 August she wrote to Mercer again, describing herself as 'surrounded by spies' and the house in Windsor as 'a perfect prison', and recounting the political manoeuvring in which she was being played as a pawn.

As for her mother, the association with the Whigs was no more than expediency. When the Tories were in opposition, the Tories had been her advisers. Now that the Whigs were in opposition, her advisers were the Whigs.

The two closest of these were the brilliant but unscrupulous Scottish lawyer Henry Brougham and a rich, vulgar brewer's son, Samuel Whitbread. Like the Tories they leaked little stories to the press, representing the Princess of Wales in the best light they could, and her husband, which was easier, in the worst; and they waited patiently for the opportunity to manipulate the relationship to their best possible advantage. It was not a long wait.

Early in October Charlotte went up from Windsor for one of her now rare visits to her mother at Kensington Palace. Since Lady de Clifford was suffering from an eye infection, she was escorted by one of the Queen's lady companions.

Before they left the Queen gave her companion, Miss Cornelia Knight, strict instructions. 'Do not let Princess Charlotte go out of your sight for one moment.'

She was equally firm with her granddaughter, telling her 'not to retire at all', to which Charlotte answered understandably that she would have to retire to change for dinner and that there was nothing she had to say to her mother that she was not prepared to say in front of anybody else.

But by then the Queen's caution was no longer necessary. A few weeks earlier Lieutenant Hesse had sailed with his regiment for Spain.

In the following week the Princess of Wales wrote to the Queen demanding that her daughter should be allowed to visit her more often and threatening to come down to Windsor unannounced if she was not. On the advice of Brougham and Whitbread, who probably wrote the letter for her, she sent a copy to Charlotte.

Innocently, Charlotte told her grandmother. The Queen, who had decided to ignore the letter, was concerned to learn that there was a copy of it. She sent for the Prince Regent. The Prince Regent sent for the Prime Minister. When Charlotte was summoned she told them that she had burned the letter. Somehow, the Prime Minister managed to persuade the Prince and his mother that they were worrying about nothing, and that there was nothing they could do about it anyway.

A week later, however, when Charlotte went on her scheduled fortnightly visit to Kensington Palace, her mother persuaded her to tell her everything that had been said at the meeting. When Charlotte seemed apprehensive, her mother reassured her. 'She did nothing without good advice.' And then, after another week, to Charlotte's bitter amazement, her 'accurate' account of the family row appeared in several newspapers.

Using Charlotte and her mother, the Whigs had succeeded in reducing the Regent still further in the eyes of the people. They had forgotten the earlier rumours about the Princess of Wales. To them she was now a thwarted mother as well as an abandoned wife, and the Prince Regent was more than ever a decadent bully.

After that, when Charlotte drove out in her carriage, she was greeted with shouts of 'Don't desert your mother, dear!'

❋

In December, when the Prince Regent was due to open Parliament, he agreed reluctantly that it would look bad if he did not invite his daughter to attend. After the ceremony and the speech from the throne, he came out and drove back to Carlton House, through crowds that were at best silent but more often jeered or shouted, 'Down with the Regent!' Behind him his daughter drove waving through a wall of cheers and chants of 'Charlotte! Charlotte! Charlotte!'

By the time the Princess reached Warwick House, she can have been in no doubt. She was now the most popular member of the royal family.

Soon afterwards Lady de Clifford resigned as governess. The continuing eye infection was a good excuse, but she must have known that her lack of vigilance had lost her the confidence of her employer, and that it was probably better to jump before she was pushed. On top of that she felt betrayed by the Prince Regent. When, in accordance with what she saw as her duty, she had passed on information 'respecting the conduct of a person known to His Royal Highness', he had promised not to repeat it. But it was now quite clear that he had broken his promise.

When the Regent asked her why she was resigning so suddenly, Lady de Clifford replied, 'Because your Royal Highness has taught me the distinction between the word of honour of a Prince and a gentleman.'

It was a mistake to insult a man who was known to be a great bearer of grudges. Some months later, to her surprise, the Prince invited Lady de Clifford to a ball. Foolishly she accepted. When the evening came the Prince walked up the group of guests among whom she was standing, greeted everyone else and then turned his back on the crestfallen Lady de Clifford.

As usual Charlotte was only told that Lady de Clifford had resigned on grounds of ill health. Around Christmas she wrote to her innocently at length, telling her how much she missed her, reporting that the Duke of Brunswick had shaved off his moustache and that her father had given her a white Italian greyhound, and ending 'God bless you, my dearest Lady.'

In January 1813, just after she had celebrated her seventeenth birthday, Charlotte was told that her new governess was to be the Duchess of Leeds and that, since Mrs Udney had also decided to retire, her new sub-governess was to be Miss Cornelia Knight.

Charlotte was furious. No girl of seventeen had a governess. And anyway she was a princess. She ought to have her own establishment by now. She ought to have ladies-in-waiting. And one of them ought to be Mercer Elphinstone.

But this was never an argument that was going to have any effect on her father. In the last of several heated meetings, in the presence of the Queen and the Lord Chancellor, who had been brought along to add legal weight to the Prince's prejudices, he informed his daughter that the best he was prepared to do would be to describe Miss Knight as a 'lady companion' and not a 'sub-governess'.

'Besides' he said, with all the self-deluding confidence of someone who barely knows the half of it, 'I know all that passed in Windsor Park; and if it were not for my clemency, I would shut you up for life. Depend upon it, as long as I live you shall never have an establishment, unless you marry.'

The Prince Regent was still determined to treat his daughter as a child. But there was not another man in the kingdom who felt inclined to do the same.

Five months later, over eight hundred miles away, Wellington defeated the French at Vittoria and prepared to drive them back over the mountains into France. According to Captain Gronow of the 1st Foot Guards, one of the officers wounded in that battle was Lieutenant Charles Hesse of the 18th, who received his first slash on his sword arm. While he was recovering, Hesse was honoured by a visit from Wellington himself. The General gave him a package that had been sent out from London, apparently by 'a royal lady'. It contained a beautiful gold watch, a hunter, and there was a portrait of the lady inside the cover.

CHAPTER SIX

'Protracted Childhood'

———

'DEPEND UPON IT, as long as I live you shall never have an establishment, unless you marry.'

The Prince Regent did not always mean what he said, but Princess Charlotte knew all too well that he had been serious when he said that. For her, marriage was the price of freedom. If that was not enough of an incentive to marry the first man who asked her, the regime of the Duchess of Leeds was another.

It was not that the Duchess was in any way strict. On the contrary, she was easy-going and avoided every kind of conflict. She concurred with 'the Great UP' at every opportunity. When Charlotte was in London, she only came to Warwick House between 2 and 5 p.m., which gave the Princess the evenings to herself. But she was a boring, graceless, self-important hypochondriac. She was forever telling 'stories of an hour's length' and taking cold showers to wash away her latest ailment. Worst of all, in Charlotte's eyes, she was 'a violent Tory'.

The daughter of the Accountant-General to the Court of Chancery, the Duchess had won her Duke's heart on the basis of her beauty alone, and her exalted new rank had gone to her head. To Charlotte's embarrassment, she often 'overacted' her part and was patronising with people whom she regarded as inferiors.

Even so, the Duchess's 'disagreeable' company might have been worth suffering if her easy-going nature had allowed Charlotte to meet and correspond with anyone she pleased. But protecting the Princess from undesirable influences was the one duty that she tried to take seriously. She was always, as Charlotte put it, 'keeping close' to her in public, and, with an air of innocence, the Duchess introduced her fifteen-year-old daughter, Lady Catherine Osborne, into Charlotte's household.

To everyone outside that household, it seemed ideal that the Princess should have a companion closer to her own age. It does not seem to have occurred to any of them that a fifteen-year-old girl who danced well had nothing in common with a sophisticated seventeen-year-old Princess who looked and behaved as though she were at least twenty. But the people who were actually members of that household were very soon suspicious of Lady Catherine. She asked too many questions, and she was all too often found alone in Charlotte's room without a good reason for being there. As Charlotte wrote to Mercer, 'That odious Lady Catherine is a <u>convenient spie</u> upon everybody in the house, with her <u>long nose</u> of bad omen, & her <u>flippant</u> way of walking <u>so lightly</u> that one never hears her.'

Things were not as bad as they could have been, however. The tedious Duchess and her prying daughter were effectively thwarted by the conspiratorial loyalty of Miss Cornelia Knight.

'The Chevalier', as Charlotte called her, was, like Mercer, the daughter of an admiral. As a child she had met many of England's leading authors and artists, including Dr Johnson, Oliver Goldsmith and Sir Joshua Reynolds. After her father's death she and her mother had lived for many years in Italy, where she wrote several books, including a guide to the Roman countryside, *Latium*, and a historical novel, *Marcus Flaminius*. When her mother died the almost penniless Miss Knight was offered a home at the British Embassy in Naples by Sir William and Lady Hamilton, and on her return to England she was appointed a lady companion to the Queen on the recommendation of the novelist Fanny Burney, who was also one of Her Majesty's ladies.

At the end of her entertaining life Cornelia Knight published a long, revealing memoir. But until the day she sat down to write it she was resolutely discreet. She had lived in Naples at a time when Lady Hamilton was conducting her notorious affair with Lord Nelson, and yet she insisted that 'the attention paid to Lord Nelson appeared perfectly natural'. It was she who checked regularly and caught Lady Catherine so often in Charlotte's room. Like Mercer, she was a true friend and confidante to the Princess. She was the most reliable of the couriers who carried letters between them, and when the need for security called for it, she even wrote some of the letters herself.

From the moment she set foot in Warwick House, which was, she wrote, 'falling to ruins', Cornelia Knight was overwhelmed with sentimental sympathy for Charlotte. When she first went with her to dine with her father at Carlton House, she was initially flattered by the warmth of his greeting and then disillusioned by the way in which he patronised and ignored his daughter. A few days later, at a small gathering in the Duke of York's apartments, her disillusion turned to indignation when she discovered that she was expected to be as much of a spy and a guardian as the Duchess.

As he shook her hand in greeting, the Prince Regent asked her in a whisper to remember what his sister Princess Mary had said to her.

Since the Princess had not spoken to her, a bewildered Miss Knight went up to Her Royal Highness later in the evening and asked what her brother had meant.

'Oh, nothing', said Princess Mary. 'He is only afraid lest Charlotte should like the Duke of Gloucester; and there is no danger. He wanted me to set you on your guard.'

After that Cornelia Knight could be in no doubt about the Regent's intentions. 'Every consideration', she wrote, 'was to be sacrificed to the plan of keeping the Princess Charlotte as long as possible a child; and, consequently, whoever belonged to her was to be thought a nurse or a preceptress'.

But the intellectual admiral's daughter was not the sort of person who was prepared to be thought of as a nurse or a preceptress; from then on she did all that she dared to counteract the plan.

When the *Morning Chronicle* announced that Miss Knight had been appointed 'sub-governess' to the Princess, she insisted that they retract the statement and print that she had been appointed 'lady companion'. At the age of fifty-seven she was too old to call herself a lady-in-waiting to so young a princess, but that did not prevent her from behaving like one. Whenever she accompanied the Princess in public she made it plain by her manner that she was in attendance, not in charge. There was never any of the air of self-important authority that always accompanied Mrs Udney.

Despite the policy of 'protracted childhood', however, there was one sign that the Prince Regent might be relenting a little. Two days after the exchange in the Duke of York's apartments, on 5 February, Charlotte was allowed to attend her first ball at Carlton House. The Duchess and Miss Knight went with her. In accordance with fashion, they were 'all in white'. The Duchess and Miss Knight wore white trimmed with gold. Charlotte wore white trimmed with silver, and for the first time, again in the height of fashion, she wore ostrich feathers in her hair.

For Charlotte, the ball was a bit of a disappointment. She had been led to believe that it was being given for her, but when the time came it was Princess Mary and not Charlotte who was asked to lead off the dancing. She had hoped that she would be able to dance with the young Duke of Devonshire, but soon after she arrived she was told that he was indisposed.

The son of the famously beautiful Duchess, Georgiana, the 23-

year-old Duke of Devonshire was very deaf and consequently shy and silent. Charlotte had 'liked him very much' when she first met him. She was proud that she had put him at his ease and induced him to 'talk a great deal'. But she was not attracted to him. As she told Mercer, 'he is certainly very plain'.

Nevertheless, as with the Duke of Gloucester, Charlotte's father was worried by his apparent interest in her, and particularly so in this case because the Duke of Devonshire was a leading Whig. 'Really the Prince Regent is so excessively tiresome & absurd about everything of that sort', she wrote to Mercer, '...& he is so suspicious always about my politics'. It may be therefore that the Duke was not present because the Prince had told him to stay away.

Without the young Duke, Charlotte could only dance with her uncles and other, much older, partners. As one of the other guests, Miss Mary Berry, put it, 'all very magnificent, but such a lack of dancing young men and, indeed, women, I quite pitied the Princess Charlotte from the bottom of my heart for the dulness of the ball'.

But this, at least, was not due to any exaggerated caution on the part of the Prince Regent. There was a dearth of good dancing partners in London in 1813. Like George FitzClarence and Charles Hesse, most of the young men worth dancing with were serving with Wellington in Spain.

Cornelia Knight enjoyed the ball even less than the Princess. In the course of the evening the Prince Regent took her aside and subjected her to a long, detailed and embarrassing diatribe against his wife. At the end of it he 'even accused her of threatening to declare that Princess Charlotte was not his daughter'.

Miss Knight was 'horrified'. 'I really knew not what to answer.'

In the light of what happened next, it is possible that the Prince Regent was trying to earn Miss Knight's sympathy, so that she, and hopefully his daughter, would be on his side when the storm broke.

CHAPTER SEVEN

'Infamous Insinuations'

———

ON 10 FEBRUARY the *Morning Chronicle* printed a letter that had been written by Charlotte's mother to her father.

In it the Princess of Wales complained at length about the injustice of reducing her meetings with her daughter from one a week to one a fortnight. The 'Delicate Investigation' had been unable to substantiate any of the charges against her, and yet, by limiting her contact with Charlotte and thereby treating her as though she were a corrupting influence, the Prince Regent was implying to the world that she was guilty of all of them.

In one paragraph she wrote, 'Let me implore you to reflect on the situation in which I am placed: without the shadow of a charge against me; without even an accuser; after an inquiry that led to my ample vindication, yet treated as if I were still more culpable than the perjuries of my suborned traducers represented me, holding me up to the world as a mother who may not enjoy the society of her only child.'

When he first received this letter, the Prince Regent had returned it unopened. The Princess of Wales had then sent it to the Prime

Minister and the Lord Chancellor, who also returned it unopened. When she sent it a second time to her husband, he read it but did not deign to answer. After that, in what she saw as justified exasperation, she had decided to put her case before the people and asked the *Morning Chronicle* to publish it.

But, as she admitted herself in the opening paragraph, her letter concerned matters that were more personal than public. Even the Prince Regent was taken aback when her next step was to publish without warning.

He went round to Warwick House accompanied by the Prime Minister, Lord Liverpool. While Miss Knight waited with an embarrassed Lord Liverpool in the dingy Library, the Prince Regent went upstairs to the drawing-room with Charlotte. 'The scene', she wrote afterwards, was 'most painful'. Her father spoke of her mother in 'constant strong language'. As a result of the letter, her mother's conduct would have to be investigated again. For the time being, therefore, Charlotte was forbidden to see her at all, and for the sake of appearances she must spend more time with her father. But apart from that, he told her callously, her life would not be affected in any way. There was no need to worry. She could go to as many balls as she wanted.

When he had finished, the Prince summoned Lord Liverpool and Miss Knight and, on the grounds that he regarded them as 'his confidential servant' and 'Princess Charlotte's friend', tactlessly repeated everything that he had just said to his daughter.

Afterwards, when the Prince and Miss Knight were alone in the library, he asked her why Charlotte had seemed so upset by this. She had taken it all 'perfectly well' when they were alone together. 'The Chevalier' turned on her Prince. What Her Royal Highness was prepared to hear from him alone, she told him, was not necessarily something she was prepared to hear in front of 'persons unconnected with the family'.

Charlotte was mortified. But she was not deceived. As she told

Mercer Elphinstone, the Prince and his Tory friends were wrong if they thought they had 'gained me over to their side by promising me gaities'.

As for her mother's letter, she saw it for what it was. It was not the plea of a neglected parent. Nor was it another protest of innocence from a woman who had been wronged. It was simply a piece of political vengeance. Although the *Chronicle* claimed that the letter was written in her mother's hand, it was clear from the pomposity of the language that the real author was Henry Brougham.

Charlotte's father had risen to the bait, and as always he was handling the crisis badly. But she could find no fault with her muddleheaded mother. This time at least the blame lay with the man who was manipulating her. Despite her respect for Brougham as 'a very able man', Charlotte was scathing in her contempt for what he had done. To have published the letter in his own interest 'to be bought for 6 pence in every shop' was in her view 'stooping very low'.

✳

Over the next three weeks, while the press and the gossips speculated again, the conclusions of the 'Delicate Investigation' were circulated and discussed among all the members of the Privy Council.

Throughout it all Charlotte lived very quietly. For the first ten days she never ventured beyond the garden of Warwick House. The promised balls never materialised, and she would not have gone to them if they had. She did not believe that it would be appropriate to be seen in pubic while her mother was 'under a cloud'. She declined politely when Lady Liverpool suggested that she should go to the theatre or the opera. She even refused when the royal doctor, Sir Henry Halford, told her that it would be better for her health if she took the air in her carriage occasionally.

But then, on the morning of 22 February, she received a visit from the Hervey sisters, who warned her about the latest gossip. It was being said that the Princess was not showing herself in public because she was pregnant, and that the father was Captain Fitz-Clarence. After that Charlotte and Cornelia Knight went out almost every day in her carriage and drove up and down for an hour or two in the Mall.

On 1 March they returned from their drive to find that the Duchess of Leeds had been summoned to Carlton House. When she came back she told Miss Knight that the deliberations of the Privy Council had 'finished dreadfully'. A paper was to be sent at eight o'clock that evening, and the Duchess was under orders to read it aloud to Charlotte and Miss Knight.

At eight the paper duly arrived, sealed and addressed to the Duchess of Leeds. The Duchess handed it unopened to Charlotte.

From that delicate moment onwards, Charlotte's opinion of the Duchess changed. She still resented her regime, and she still found her company 'disagreeable'. But she no longer disliked her.

Charlotte read the paper. 'I have no objection to anyone hearing this', she said.

According to Cornelia Knight, she then read it out loud to them. It was nothing more than the Privy Council's re-wording of the report from 'The Delicate Investigation', together with the conclusion that in the light of this the Prince Regent was justified in limiting his daughter's visits to her mother.

Judging by what Charlotte wrote to Mercer next day, she does not seem to have known much about the original investigation. The document, she wrote, was merely a 'vague & incomprehensible & undefined' answer to her mother's letter, although towards the end it contained 'most insidious & infamous insinuations'.

As for her father's threat that she should no longer be allowed to see her mother, 'it <u>does not say a word against it</u>, but only that my visits should be subjected to <u>restrictions & limitations</u> as usual'. 'After all this farce', she added, 'it leaves you just where you were before'.

But the continuing farce did not leave the Prince Regent just where he was before.

Urged on by her Whig advisers, his wife milked the situation for all it was worth. She wrote to the Speaker of the House of Commons demanding that Parliament should pass a motion exonerating her from all the unfounded charges that her husband had laid against her.

For the first three weeks of March the original findings of 'The Delicate Investigation' were debated in the House of Commons. Whitbread spoke passionately and at length. Several members proposed that the Douglases should be charged with perjury. But eventually, when the Whigs realised that they could not push the embarrassed government any further without seeming sanctimonious, the debates petered out inconclusively.

Outside Parliament, on the other hand, the discussion continued for some time. The investigation's findings were now public knowledge. In the little world of society gossips they provided fuel for further salacious speculation. But to the press and the people at large they were just more evidence that the Prince Regent was a scoundrel. To them, his wife was a heroine who had borne his calumnies with commendable courage. She was cheered and clapped wherever she went; and she went everywhere she could to make the most of it.

Using the most sinister of his many raffish friends as go-betweens, the Prince Regent tried to bribe or bully some of the newspapers into printing an attack on his wife's character. But he was rebuffed so disdainfully that he was lucky not to be exposed for it. His only successful vengeance lay in continuing to prevent his wife from seeing his daughter.

They did meet once fortuitously, when their carriages passed each other in the street. Ordering their drivers to halt as they drew level, they leaned out of the windows to embrace and then stayed there talking for several minutes while the people on the pavements clapped. Despite this additional humiliation for the Prince, there were also two occasions on which he relented and allowed Charlotte a brief visit to her mother. One was when she went to take her a present on her birthday. The other was when she went to offer unnecessary consolation after the unlamented death of the old Duchess of Brunswick.

✳

For Charlotte the spring and summer of 1813 were for the most part dreary and sad. The only balls that she attended were in the houses of her father or her uncles, and at all of them the Prince Regent was as paranoid as ever.

At one ball, given by the Duke and Duchess of York, the Prince saw that his daughter was again sitting on a sofa talking to the Duke of Gloucester, for whom, if he only knew it, she did not have 'the smallest partiality'. He instructed Lady Liverpool to go over and tell her to change places with Lady Bathurst, who was sitting on the other side of her. Instead of obeying, Charlotte stood up and strode out of the room. Later she went back and apologised to the Duke, and she went home, in the words of Cornelia Knight, 'indignant and hurt at having been watched and worried'.

The Prince was equally suspicious of the Duke of Devonshire, who was certainly very attentive to Charlotte. But, as she told Mercer, she only wished he would bestow his attentions somewhere else, where they might at least be appreciated. Sir Henry Halford, who was fast becoming the Prince's favourite messenger, was sent more than once to admonish the Duchess of Leeds and Miss Knight for not keeping a close enough watch when the Duke of Devonshire was around. And on another occasion he was sent to tell Miss Knight that the Prince was not pleased to learn that she and Charlotte had been seen out in her carriage one morning on the road to Chiswick, where the Duke was giving a breakfast party at his villa – to which Miss Knight pleaded honestly that life at Warwick House was so dull that they had simply gone out to watch all the fancy carriages drive by.

The Prince even forbade Charlotte to continue sitting for the painter George Sanders at his studio, because while she was there she was exposed to the bad influence of such visitors as Lady Jersey. Both the Duchess of Leeds and Miss Knight insisted defiantly that the pious painter and his studio were beyond reproach. Charlotte was having her portrait painted as a birthday present for her father, and the visitors were only there to see how it was coming on, sometimes at the Prince's request. But it was to no avail, and since Sanders refused to paint at Warwick House, where the light was as bad as everything else, the birthday present was never finished.

※

Throughout all this Charlotte spent a large part of every day nursing Mrs Gagarin. She had not been well for several months, and by the end of March it seemed likely that she would not recover.

'While she was capable of taking airings', wrote Cornelia Knight, 'her Royal Highness constantly sent her out in a carriage, and when she grew so weak as to be confined to her room, visited her two or three times a day, carried her in her arms to the window, and exerted every faculty to soothe and comfort her.'

Her death was recorded in the *Gentleman's Magazine*:

'July 1. At Warwick House, Mrs Gagarin, many years an affectionate and faithful attendant of the Princess Charlotte of Wales. Her last moments were solaced by the condescending and unremitting attentions of her Royal Highness, reflecting a lustre on the native goodness of her heart, superior to all the appendages of her exalted rank.'

Charlotte, wrote Miss Knight, 'was very low for a long time afterwards, though she endeavoured to suppress and conceal her feelings'.

Yet amid all this sadness and frustration there was one element of happiness – the presence of Mercer Elphinstone.

Mercer came down from Scotland in the middle of March and stayed until the end of July.

When she knew her friend was coming, Charlotte wrote to her father, saying that she had heard the news from a third party and asking his permission to see her. Their correspondence had been, as Charlotte put it, 'conducted with such secrecy & prudence' that the Prince was convinced they had not been in touch with each other. All Charlotte's letters were still being opened by his agents at the Post Office, and there had been no sign of it. He therefore acceded to what he regarded as a reasonable request.

There were some, including Cornelia Knight, who suspected that the Prince had written to Mercer saying that he would only let her see his daughter if she promised to persuade her not to be too supportive of her mother. But Mercer, who was always wary of Charlotte's mother, would have done that anyway if she thought it appropriate.

For more than four months Charlotte and Mercer saw each other as often as they pleased. But the Prince Regent had forbidden Mercer to stay in the same house as Charlotte. So when Charlotte was in London, Mercer came round to Warwick House from her own house in Harley Street, and when Charlotte was in Windsor at Lower Lodge, Cornelia Knight arranged for Mercer to stay nearby with a friend, Mrs Hallam.

Throughout those months there were no letters. There is therefore no record of what they discussed. But there is no doubt that one of the most important topics was the rumour that Mercer mentioned in one of her last letters from Scotland.

In her reply Charlotte wrote that she too had heard it. Perhaps, if the Princess were willing to pay it, the price of freedom would soon be available.

It was being said that the Prince Regent and his ministers were planning to arrange a marriage between Princess Charlotte and the Hereditary Prince of Orange.

CHAPTER EIGHT

'Slender Billy'

———

BACK IN 1795, while Charlotte's mother and Lord Malmesbury were held up in Hanover by the fighting in Holland, the Dutch Stadholder and his family had escaped to England. But his eldest son, Prince William VI, who succeeded him as head of the House of Orange in 1806, did not like England or the English. He blamed his British allies for abandoning his army as soon as the French returned to the attack. After only a few months in London, he left for Prussia, where he spent the next twelve years attempting to ingratiate himself with Napoleon.

Since Napoleon had made his brother Louis King of Holland, it was never likely that he was going to give it back to the House of Orange; in 1807 Prince William realised at last that it would be wiser to hedge his bets. He may not have liked it, but he had to accept that, if Napoleon were ever to be defeated, the people who were most likely to help him were the British. He approached Lord Malmesbury, who had once been British Ambassador at The Hague, and suggested that the natural alliance between Holland and England should be strengthened by a marriage between his son and heir, known as the Hereditary Prince of Orange, and the heir presumptive to the throne of England, Princess Charlotte.

Malmesbury could see the benefits. Britain's security would be greatly enhanced if the state that lay between England and Hanover were tied irrevocably to the British crown, and if the Dutch fleet were to be combined with the Royal Navy, Britannia's rule of the waves would be unassailable. It was a good idea, and it was not, after all, a new idea. At the end of the seventeenth century the son of the Stadholder had married the daughter of the King of England, and they had ruled England jointly as William and Mary.

Encouraged by Malmesbury, the Dutch Prince decided to prepare his son for this possible opportunity by sending him to Oxford to get an English education. In 1811, after Charlotte's father had become Regent, the Prince of Orange flattered him by consulting him about his son's future: it was agreed that the young man, now twenty years old, should be commissioned into the British army. So when he came down from Oxford, the Hereditary Prince of Orange went out to Spain, to serve as an aide-de-camp to Wellington.

By the spring of 1813 the tide had turned against Napoleon. Everywhere his armies were falling back towards France. In the north, the Russians and Prussians were driving them southwards. In the south, Wellington and his allies were driving them northwards. The monarchs and statesmen of Europe were beginning to plan for the peace that was now within their grasp.

From the British point of view, the best way to maintain that peace was to create a strong 'buffer state' separating France from Prussia, and the ideal state for that was Holland. But Holland would have to be strong enough to withstand any initial threat, and stable enough to remain reliable. To make it strong enough, why not increase its size by incorporating part of the Austrian Netherlands, in the area that is now Belgium? To make it stable, why not give it a constitutional monarchy, like England's, and make the Prince of Orange a king instead of just a stadholder? And to extend the buffer

even further, and make the new state susceptible to British influence, why not arrange a marriage between neighbours – between the
ruling families of Holland and Hanover?

So that was the plan. The Prince of Orange was delighted. He was
going to be a king, and king of an enlarged kingdom as well. It was
more than he could have dreamed possible.

But so far no one had bothered to mention it to the future Queen
of England or the Prince who might one day succeed his father as
King William II of Holland.

Nevertheless there were too many whispers. Charlotte was sure
that the plan was true, and she was in two minds about it. On the
one hand the Hereditary Prince of Orange came from a family that
her mother 'detested', and Charlotte would never 'be tempted to
purchase temporary ease by gratifying the Windsor & Ministerial
cabals'. On the other hand, if the Prince had enough 'qualities of
the head & heart' to make him 'likeable and desirable', he offered a
chance to change her life for the better, even if 'love' was 'out of the
question'.

All that was certain for the time being was that Charlotte was
prepared to give the plan a chance. But her first experience of the
House of Orange did not leave her with a good impression.

It was on 12 August, at the Prince Regent's birthday party – the
one to which Charlotte went without a present. The party was held at
Sandhurst, the new home of the Military Academy. In the morning
'the Great UP', now Bishop of Salisbury, consecrated the chapel, and
the Queen presented new colours to the cadets. In the evening, the
entire company sat down to dinner. The royal family and the guests
of honour, including the Prince of Orange, who was in England to
negotiate his son's future, sat at a table inside the house, and all the
other guests sat in tents in the grounds.

According to Charlotte, the only man in the royal party who was
not 'dead drunk' was her favourite uncle, the Duke of Brunswick.
In the course of the evening the Prince Regent slid silently under

the table, where he was eventually joined by the Prince of Orange, the Commander in Chief and almost all his ministers. By the time they got there, the dishevelled Prince of Orange had managed to discard his coat and waistcoat, most of the ministers were incapable of speaking and the Prime Minister, Lord Liverpool, was in such a state that, by his own admission, he could not remember next day where he had been or who he had been with.

The last to fall was the Commander in Chief, the Duke of York, who did so by rolling backwards out of his chair, banging his head against a wine cooler and pulling the table cloth and everything on it on top of him. He was revived by the Duke of Brunswick, who poured iced water over his head, and he was then sent back to London in a post-chaise, wrapped in a greatcoat.

When the Queen left, she was kept waiting for 'a full half hour' while various nervous equerries searched for her host and helped him out to see her into her carriage.

In Charlotte's opinion, the double celebration of the opening of Sandhurst and the Prince Regent's birthday 'began badly and ended in tragedy'. Miss Knight agreed. 'It was a sad business. We went home very quietly in an open carriage by the lovely moonlight.'

❉

Two days later Charlotte described the chaos in a letter to Mercer, who was now back in Scotland, and two days after that she wrote again, reporting that Wellington had defeated the French in the Pyrenees and was advancing into France, and that the news had been brought to London by the Hereditary Prince of Orange.

Charlotte was sure that the Prince had been summoned to meet her, and in support of this she recounted a conversation that had taken place between her and 'a Government person' at Windsor. According to this unnamed minister, it was being said that Charlotte had 'persistently refused' to consider her planned marriage to the Hereditary Prince of Orange.

Charlotte was incensed by his impertinence and infuriated to learn that she was already being blamed for her response to a plan that had not yet even been put to her. So she decided to tease the minister and add a red herring to his rumour. Without denying what he had said, she told him that she much preferred the Duke of Gloucester.

'Good God', said he. 'I can hardly believe you are serious.'

When he then reminded her that she could not marry without her father's permission, Charlotte answered that 'nothing was so easy as to make a publick declaration that I never would marry anyone else'.

The trick worked. The 'Government person' was clearly 'both surprised & frightened'.

'I was rather amused I confess', wrote Charlotte, and she 'laughed heartily' after he was gone.

But in reality she felt threatened. Even the government was gossiping. She went on the defensive. She declined to attend every event at which she thought the Hereditary Prince of Orange might be present. But she was curious enough to ask about him, and she learned a bit from one of his dancing partners, Georgiana Fitzroy. The Hereditary Prince was apparently 'very gentlemanlike, well informed & pleasant' and he was 'the best waltzer that ever was'. But he was also 'excessively plain' and 'thin as a needle'. Georgiana thought that Charlotte would find him 'frightful'.

Had Charlotte but known it, the Hereditary Prince was as apprehensive as she was. It was a relief to both of them when he went back to Spain after less than a month without being introduced to her. But she still felt that the plan was brewing, and she knew that she was being watched more closely than ever. Lady Catherine Osborne was everywhere. For a while Charlotte and Miss Knight had avoided being understood by her by talking to each other in

German. But Lady Catherine, who had her own governess, had learned enough German to make out what they were saying. So now they were talking to each other in Italian, and Lady Catherine was busy learning that from a music master.

One night, when Charlotte found 'her little Ladyship' loitering yet again in a dark passage, she lost patience, pushed her into the water closet, locked the door and kept her there for a quarter of an hour. 'It did for a good laugh to Miss K & me', she told Mercer, 'as the young ladies dismay was not small, & her <u>assurances</u> thro' the door <u>very amusing</u>'.

At last, on 14 October, while Charlotte was still isolated at Windsor, she had her first 'sounding out' about marriage. It came from Sir Henry Halford, who spent 'a full hour and a half' with her, asking her opinion and praising the Hereditary Prince of Orange.

Charlotte could see that things were 'coming to a crisis', but she was a long way from being ready to commit herself. She tried a trick that she had tried before. She told the doctor that she was 'resolved firmly' not to accept the Hereditary Prince of Orange and that she much preferred the Duke of Gloucester, who was after all an Englishman.

The trick worked again. Sir Henry believed her. When he took his leave, he told her solemnly that he would have to report all that she had said to her father.

As she told Mercer, Charlotte would have much preferred this to have happened when she was back in London, where it would be easier to get good advice. But she shrewdly wrote to the leader of the opposition, Earl Grey, asking him to tell her what to do.

Four days later the Prince Regent appeared at Lower Lodge. Since Charlotte had to change for dinner at Windsor Castle as soon as he left, Cornelia Knight wrote to Mercer that evening to tell her what had been said, and Charlotte followed with her own letter next day.

They were both 'shocked & disgusted' by the language that the

Prince used to describe the Duke of Gloucester, despite the persistent protesting of Miss Knight. 'It was so excessively indecent', wrote Charlotte, 'that I hardly knew which way to look'. They were also indignant when he accused his daughter of being regularly drunk, and then added that she could not possibly have fallen for the Duke of Gloucester if she had not been. But they were amused when he suggested that her affection for the Duke Gloucester might just be a ruse to disguise her true and equally unacceptable fancy for the Duke of Devonshire. And they were both suspicious at the end when he became magnanimous. There were plenty of eligible princes to choose from, he said, and then assured them that he was not the sort of man who would force his daughter to marry anyone against her will.

'The <u>fluency</u> with which he <u>utter'd falsehoods</u>' left Charlotte 'convinced that there does not live one who is a greater coward or a greater hypocrite'. But, as Mercer had advised, she held her tongue.

Next day, a long letter arrived from Earl Grey. The leader of the opposition's advice to Charlotte was to do what she was doing already – play for time.

There was only so much time left to play for, however. Charlotte knew that she would have to make some sort of decision soon. The word was out. The Gloucester story was common knowledge. The marriage of the Princess Charlotte of Wales had replaced the relationship between her parents as the principal topic for gossip. Several newspapers were asking, 'Will she choose the Orange or the Cheese – "Slender Billy" or "Silly Billy"?'

Yet there were plenty among the people and the press who still favoured the Duke of Devonshire rumour. Several journalists and cartoonists had suggested that the Regent and the Tories were offering Charlotte to the young Duke in order to tempt him and his money away from the Whigs.

The story that the Princess had fallen for the Duke of Devonshire was strengthened by Lady Charlotte Campbell, who said that there was a portrait that looked very like him hanging on a wall in Warwick House. Although Miss Knight told her that it was not the Duke, Lady Charlotte insisted to everyone that it was, and indeed it may have been, or at least it may have looked like him. In her memoir, Cornelia Knight mentioned that there was a print of one of the Dukes of Devonshire hanging among many others at Warwick House. But Lady Charlotte was not very good at guessing the subject of portraits. There was also a miniature of a young hussar in Warwick House, which the Princess said belonged to her father, but which Lady Charlotte reckoned was probably George FitzClarence, and in that she was almost certainly wrong. If the Princess owned a portrait of an unnamed hussar, he was more likely to be Charles Hesse.

※

Princess Charlotte had not yet completely recovered from her 'unfortunate folly'. On one occasion she wrote to Mercer,

> I feel rather uncomfortable I confess about an engagement I see by today's papers that has taken place between the French and the 18th Hussars in wh. two Capts & a Major I know are killed and wounded, & it says that two subaltern officers are killed also. Were anything to happen to our friend I should feel it excessively, as it is impossible not to do for a person one has been so intimate with.

But the folly was also a problem now. As Mercer pointed out, if Charlotte decided to marry her Prince, and if her mother continued to oppose the wedding, she was not above trying to stop it by revealing her daughter's relationship with Charles Hesse. And if she needed evidence to prove her story, she could probably persuade the little hussar to part with some of Charlotte's letters and presents.

When Hesse set out for Spain, he and Charlotte had agreed to burn all their letters to each other, and Charlotte had done so with his, 'for certainly they were much <u>too full</u> of <u>professions & nonsense</u> not to have got him into a desperate scrape if ever seen'. But she was pretty sure that he had not done the same thing with hers. So by the time Charlotte returned to London, at the beginning of November, Mercer had written to Lieutenant Hesse, asking him, as a man of honour, to send back everything that Charlotte had ever given or sent to him.

By then it was clear that the reign of Napoleon Bonaparte was drawing to a close. He had been defeated at Leipzig by the armies of Russia, Prussia, Sweden and Austria. Wellington had invaded France. Charlotte's favourite uncle and his Black Brunswickers had recovered their duchy. The Russian cavalry had reached Holland and the French army of occupation was withdrawing ahead of them. Napoleon's brother was no longer its king.

Not surprisingly, therefore, at the end of the month, Charlotte wrote to Mercer, 'My <u>torments & plagues</u> are again beginning <u>again spite of all</u> promises made at Windsor. I have had a <u>violent orange</u> attack this morning.'

'The little baroneted doctor' was on the offensive again. The Hereditary Prince of Orange was returning from France to Holland. He would be passing through England. The Prince Regent was planning a dinner for him. It was now Charlotte's duty to meet him and consider a marriage that could play such a vital part in the security of the realm. In pressing his case, the doctor reminded her that the marriage would bring her 'power, riches and liberty'. He had an answer for every objection. If the Prince was too thin, he could fill out. If he had bad teeth, they could be fixed.

The Prince Regent joined the campaign, but this time in a different way. He was more respectful and warm-hearted with his daughter than ever before. Twice in the course of the next week he invited her to dine at Carlton House with his most distinguished guests, among them Prince Lieven, the Russian Ambassador; Lord Castlereagh, his brilliant Foreign Secretary; and Madame de Staël, the greatest of France's women writers, who he knew was one of Charlotte's heroines.

Others lent their support, reminding Charlotte that there were many, including, it was said, Wellington, who had a high opinion of the young Prince of Orange.

Charlotte the young lady could be very stubborn. But Charlotte the princess had a sense of duty. On 8 December she wrote to Mercer: 'I have agreed without any demur or hesitation to see the young P. when he comes & as much as they please, because I am for doing all that is fair by them & indeed giving the young man a chance too.'

She accepted that a marriage would be greatly in the interest of both their countries, particularly since the Austrians were 'being jealous respecting their share of Holland'. But she did have one reservation. If she married the Prince she would not be prepared to accompany him when he went to Holland.

'As heiress presumptive to the Crown it is certain that I could not quit this country, as Queen of England still less. Therefore the P of O must visit his frogs solo.'

The Hereditary Prince of Orange landed at Portsmouth on 10 December. Next day Charlotte received a letter from Mercer, who had gone down to have a look at him as he came ashore. He had made a favourable impression. It was a relief. Mercer's opinion meant more than anyone's. It has, wrote Charlotte in reply, 'eased me of 100,000 worries'.

But the relief was short-lived. Next day, the day when Charlotte and the Prince were due to meet, her father came round in the morning to Warwick House and put the pressure on again. He assured Charlotte that there was nothing to be nervous about. The dinner party was to be informal and as small as possible. She was to be accompanied only by the Duchess of Leeds. But, 'he exacted a promise'. Charlotte must make up her mind that evening. After dinner she was to give him her answer 'one way or the other'.

꙰

When Charlotte set out for the dinner, dressed in 'violet satin, trimmed with black lace', she was, in Miss Knight's words, 'pale and agitated', and she went, in her own words 'with trepidation'.

Yet, as far as it could be, the evening was a success. The young Prince who would one day be King William II of the Netherlands sat on Princess Charlotte's right, with Lady Liverpool on his other side. 'He struck me as very plain', wrote Charlotte to Mercer, 'but he was so lively & animated that it quite went off... It is really singular how much we agreed together in allmost everything.'

After dinner, when many other guests arrived, the young couple walked up and down among them in the state apartments for a while. Then the Prince Regent came over, led Charlotte away to another room and asked her what she thought of the Prince.

Charlotte hesitated.

'Then it will not do?' he said.

'I do not say that', said Charlotte. 'I like his manner very well, as much as I have seen of it.'

It was hardly a firm answer 'one way or the other', but it was enough for the Prince Regent. He became as over-emotional as only he knew how. 'You make me the happiest person in the world', he said.

He called over the Prime Minister and Lady Liverpool and gave them the good news. While they congratulated the Princess, he summoned the 'quite awestruck' Prince. Then he joined the Prince's hand with his daughter's and gave them both his royal blessing. There was to be no going back now. Not if he could help it.

Cornelia Knight was waiting up for her when Charlotte returned to Warwick House. The Princess told her everything. She was now engaged to the young Prince of Orange. Miss Knight was astonished. 'I could only remark', she wrote years later, 'that she had gained a great victory over herself'.

But Charlotte was already coming to terms with what had happened. 'No, you would not say so if you were to see him', she said. 'He is by no means as disagreeable as I expected.'

Next day Miss Knight did get to see him. He came to call accompanied by Lord Bathurst. She was not over-impressed. 'I thought him particularly plain and sickly in his look, his figure very slender, his manner rather hearty and boyish, but not unpleasant in a young soldier.'

On the day after that the young Prince came again, this time accompanied by Charlotte's father. Tactfully, the Regent allowed the young couple to be alone together, although, for the sake of propriety, he and Miss Knight sat by the fire in the next room with the door open, so that they could see them.

The Regent told 'the Chevalier' that for the time being the betrothal was to be kept secret, and he then began to describe his plans for the marriage.

Suddenly they were both brought to their feet by the sound of Charlotte bursting into 'a violent fit of sobs and hysterical tears'.

The Regent had no idea what was happening. 'What!' he said. 'Is he taking his leave?'

'Not yet', said Charlotte, and then added that she was going to her room.

Tactful again, the Regent told the ladies that he and the Hereditary Prince were now late for a banquet and then hurriedly led him away.

When they were gone, Miss Knight asked Charlotte what was wrong, and she was not too surprised by the answer.

The Dutch Prince had just told the Princess that, when they were married, she would have to spend two or three months of every year in Holland.

Chapter Nine

Making the Best of it

———

THE HEREDITARY PRINCE of Orange was sympathetic. Before he left to spend Christmas in The Hague, he did all that he could to reassure Charlotte. When they were married, he told her, he would never insist that she came with him every time he went to Holland. Perhaps she would only need to come for two or three weeks in each year, and since by then she would have her own household, she could of course bring all her ladies with her.

For Charlotte it was enough for now. At least the Dutch Prince was being honest with her. Her real rage was with her father, who had trapped her into a quick decision without telling her what it entailed.

She was sure that in the long run she could rely on her Whig friends to advise and protect her. They would never allow their future queen to leave the country against her will. And in the short run, marriage with the latest William of Orange was still the only available key to freedom and a household of her own.

But it looks as though she was trying a bit too hard to persuade herself that the price was reasonable.

She wrote to Mercer. 'To say I am in love with him would be untrue & ridiculous but I will say that I think him the most natural, open & undisguised character that ever was. I am persuaded I shall have a very great regard & opinion of him wh. perhaps is better to begin with & more likely to last than love.'

Miss Knight was not so sure. She also wrote to Mercer. 'She thinks, or at least says, no one has influenced her.'

But Miss Knight was able to supply a long list of friends, uncles, aunts and ministers who, in her view, had done precisely that. Almost the only people who had not, she wrote, were the Duchess and the 'Bish-UP', although even they 'wished it sincerely' and had simply seen fit to keep 'clear of urging or advising'.

'The thing in itself may tend to her happiness', she wrote, 'but tricks and deception to bring about anything are horrid.'

And she ended gloomily, 'It remains now to make the best of it... to make her gain his confidence and he hers, and if possible to prevent their being governed by all these artful people. My great hope is that as there are so many, and of different views and interests, they may, though they joined in this, ultimately defeat each other's purposes.'

Meanwhile it was Christmas. For a few days doubts were set aside.

Charlotte went to Windsor. The company at the castle was, as expected, 'disagreeable'. But she was impressed twice: first by her father's tactful success in persuading the Queen to accept her engagement to a member of the House of Orange; secondly by the talent of an actress called Miss Smith, who came to read excerpts from the comedies, and who was, in Charlotte's opinion, 'far superior to Mrs Siddons'.

She returned to London in an optimistic mood. On 4 January, she wrote to Mercer. 'Holland is a very odd place I believe... Even now I <u>doubt</u> being <u>much</u> amused there... We <u>must see what</u> we can do to make it more <u>Londonish & dandyish</u>...'

7 January was Charlotte's eighteenth birthday, a day on which most noble ladies would have had a ball. But for Charlotte it was subdued and insignificant. In the morning she went with the Duchess to visit her mother, who had just abandoned Blackheath and Kensington Palace and was now living in Connaught House, on the north of the Bayswater Road, close to the junction with Park Lane. In allowing the visit, the Prince Regent had ruled that it must be brief and that there must be no mention of the engagement, which was probably just as well. On that particular morning, despite her undeserved popularity, the manic-depressive Princess of Wales was feeling lonely and consumed with self-pity.

In the evening Charlotte and Cornelia Knight listened to a little concert performed by her harp master and music master, and the tradesmen who supplied Warwick House came with their wives and danced in the dining room with the servants. The only members of Charlotte's family who were present were two of her uncles, the Dukes of Sussex and Kent, who came round at the very end of the evening.

Charlotte's father, who was staying with the Duke of Rutland at Belvoir Castle, was not pleased when he heard about his brothers' visit. The Duke of Sussex was a Whig, and he suspected rightly that he was advising his daughter to defy the government, and he also suspected that the Duke of Kent was encouraging her to be extravagant.

Soon after he returned to snow-covered London, suffering from a severe attack of gout, he summoned Miss Knight to Carlton House. First he complained at length and in general about the Dukes of Kent and Sussex, to which Miss Knight said nothing. Then he told her reproachfully that he had read in the newspapers that Charlotte had ordered a new carriage from the Duke of Kent's coach maker instead of from his own. To this she was able to answer that it was nothing to do with Charlotte. The coach had been ordered by the Duchess of Leeds, who had simply consulted the Duke of Kent. But she did not have such a good answer when he censured Charlotte for spending far too much on jewellery and said that he thought it shameful for young ladies of immense fortune to accept valuable gifts from his daughter – he had clearly heard about the bracelet that had been given to Mercer for Christmas. In the end, as though it was a consequence of his displeasure, he said that, since his daughter was about to be married, she must consider her duties as a wife and live without amusements for a while.

❄

So for the next two months Charlotte lived in Warwick House in dull and dignified isolation. The only notable events were the various stages in the protracted negotiations over one small clause in her marriage contract.

Lords Liverpool and Castlereagh, who were drawing up the contract, were aware of most people's reservations. They knew that no one wanted to see the crowns of England and Holland united. So they stipulated that, if Charlotte and William had more than one child, the eldest son would inherit England and the next Holland. If they had only one child, that child would inherit England and the Dutch crown would go to the German branch of the House of Orange. But, out of deference to the Dutch, the Prime Minister and the Foreign Secretary both felt that Princess Charlotte ought to be required to spend at least some time each year in Holland.

Among the Whigs there were some, such as the Duke of Sussex and Earl Grey, who approved of the proposed marriage but felt that Charlotte should never be required to leave the country against her will. But there were many others, among them Brougham and Whitbread, who were passionately opposed to the marriage. As a matter of principle they objected to turning the Dutch Republic into a monarchy, and they felt that Britain would be taking on the huge additional expense of providing for the defence of Holland, sometimes perhaps in circumstances where Britain itself was not threatened.

As a first step towards changing Charlotte's mind, Brougham tried to persuade her that her father wanted to get her out of the country because he envied her popularity.

Charlotte was susceptible to that. She was learning not to trust her father. That was one reason why the negotiations were taking so long. She insisted that everything must be in writing – partly to prevent her father from subsequently denying anything that suited him, and partly because she was sending everything to Grey and Brougham, so that they could tell her what to write in reply.

Naturally Mercer was also consulted, first by letter and then in person. She came to town in the middle of February, and after that the most reliable of all secret messengers carried the letters between Charlotte and her Whig advisers.

In the correspondence and conversations with Mercer there was, however, one other cause for concern – Lieutenant Hesse. He had written back to Mercer at last. Most of his letters and presents from Charlotte were in a trunk which he had left in the care of an un-named friend in England. In the event of his death, the friend had promised to sink the trunk and its contents in the river Thames. As for the letters and the watch that were with him, he did not think it was safe to send them back at the moment, but he would leave instructions that, if he was killed, all his possessions were to be sent to Mercer.

It was not a satisfactory answer. But it would have to do until Hesse came home, and that was likely to be soon. Everyone outside France was preparing for the end that now seemed inevitable.

❋

As soon as they were rid of Napoleon, all the European sovereigns were planning to come to England to celebrate their victory, and as a vanguard, or perhaps a reconnaissance, the Tsar's favourite sister, the Grand Duchess Catherine, arrived while Napoleon was still at large.

The clever and cultured Grand Duchess Catherine was dark and dignified with slavonic, slightly Mongolian features. At the age of twenty-five she was already a widow. After nursing her husband, Prince George of Oldenberg, through his long, fatal illness, she went to neighbouring Holland, where she met Charlotte's uncle William, the Duke of Clarence, who was there on a goodwill visit, and who was soon besotted with her.

When she announced her intention to travel on to England, the Prince Regent sent one of the Royal Navy's cutters to bring her over. But the Grand Duchess Catherine was much too grand a duchess to travel in a mere cutter, and besides she had three or four carriages with her and thirty-seven people on her staff. So Admiral His Royal Highness the Duke of Clarence, who was to be remembered as 'The Sailor King', ordered up a frigate, HMS *Jason*, and stood off himself in the cutter as an escort.

The Grand Duchess arrived in London on 17 March. At the Prince Regent's expense, she and her staff, which included her senile governess, Princess Volkonskoi and, ironically, Prince Gagarin, took over the entire Pulteney Hotel, the first in the world to have 'en suite' bathrooms, which stood opposite Green Park on the corner of Bolton Street and Piccadilly.

For the first six weeks of her stay, however, the Grand Duchess used the hotel only as a base. She visited Oxford, Cambridge, Bath and as many of the great country houses as she could manage. When she was in town she went frequently to the opera and the theatre. She was shown round the Bank of England by the directors, but she asked such penetrating technical questions that they had to send for one of the clerks to answer them. She was shown round Whitbread's brewery by Samuel Whitbread, which infuriated his former friend the Prince Regent. And to the delight of the Londoners, who adored her in no time, she drove everywhere in an open carriage wearing the huge coal-scuttle bonnet that became the model for one of the most characteristic Regency fashions.

When the Grand Duchess arrived in London, the Prince Regent went round to the hotel to welcome her. But he went much too early. She was still changing to receive him when a footman came to announce his arrival. The meeting was more embarrassing than cordial.

That evening, when she dined at Carlton House, the Grand Duchess confirmed the opinion that she had formed earlier. She did not like the Prince Regent. But she liked very much his daughter, who was also present. In a letter to her brother the Tsar she described Charlotte as 'the most interesting member of the family... She is blonde, has a handsome nose, a delicious mouth and fine teeth... She is full of spirit and positive in character. She seems to have an iron will in the smallest things...' But 'her manners', wrote the Grand Duchess, 'are so extraordinary that they take one's breath away... She walks up to any man, young or old, especially to the older men, takes them by the hand, and shakes it with all her strength... She looks like a boy, or rather a ragamuffin. I really am telling you nothing but the strictest truth. She is ravishing, and it is a crime to have allowed her to acquire such habits.'

After that dinner the Grand Duchess Catherine and Princess Charlotte visited each other often at the Pulteney Hotel and Warwick House – so often in fact that the Prince Regent sent Sir Henry Halford to Warwick House with an order for Miss Knight. She was to do all that she could to reduce the frequency of these meetings. It was an order that Miss Knight had neither the power nor the will to obey. She could cut down on Charlotte's visits to the Pulteney Hotel, but she could do nothing to prevent the Grand Duchess from coming round to Warwick House – which was fortunate. Since the Regent was preventing his daughter from appearing anywhere in society other than at Carlton House, these visits were almost the only occasions on which the Princess and the Grand Duchess were able to meet.

One evening at a dinner party given by Lord and Lady Liverpool, the Prince Regent sat with the Grand Duchess Catherine on his right and the Princess Lieven, wife of the Russian Ambassador, on his left. In the course of dinner the Grand Duchess turned to him.

'Why, your Royal Highness, do you keep your daughter under lock and key?' she asked. 'Why does she appear nowhere?'

'My daughter is too young, Madame, to appear in society', said the Prince.

'She is not too young for you to have chosen her a husband.'

The Prince was clearly uncomfortable. 'She will not be married for another two years', he said.

'When she is married', said the Grand Duchess, 'I hope she will know how to make up for her present imprisonment.'

The Prince snapped back at her. 'When she is married, Madame, she will do her husband's will, just as at present she is doing mine.'

The Grand Duchess smiled and spoke very sweetly. 'Ah, yes. Your Royal Highness is right. Between husband and wife there can only be one will.'

So far the conversation had been conducted in French. But now the Prince turned to the Princess Lieven and spoke in English, in rage, and loudly enough for everyone at the table to hear him.

'This is intolerable!'

The Grand Duchess and Charlotte continued to meet, and the Grand Duchess was always as blunt with Charlotte as she had been with her father. She told her that she thought the Prince Regent was 'a voluptuary'. And as for the Duke of Clarence, he was positively 'vulgar'. While they were in Holland he had actually been so presumptuous as to propose to her.

It was at one of these meetings, on 5 April, that Lord Bathurst called to inform Princess Charlotte that the allies had entered Paris. Four days later news came that Napoleon had abdicated.

CHAPTER TEN

'The Summer of the Tsars'

OVER THE NEXT eight weeks the Prince Regent, his staff and his government were preoccupied with planning all the balls, banquets and ceremonies that would take place in June, when most of the sovereigns and statesmen of Europe were due to assemble in London as his guests. Other than taking part in the events themselves, there was nothing he enjoyed more than organising them, and his preoccupation added further delays to the written negotiations that were still passing backwards and forwards between the splendour of Carlton House and his daughter's dingy home next door.

The Prince Regent still stubbornly insisted that Charlotte must spend some time each year in Holland, and he used every argument and every messenger in his campaign to change her mind. He even sent the Duke of York to reason with her. But Charlotte, who had not said that she would never go to Holland, still insisted equally stubbornly that she must not be forced to go against her will.

Eventually, early in the morning of 30 April, a servant went to Miss Knight and told her that there was a young officer, Captain St George, at the door. Miss Knight went down to meet him and then rushed upstairs to Charlotte, who was still in bed. The young officer was the Hereditary Prince of Orange, who had just arrived from The Hague, travelling incognito.

Someone had clearly sent for him in the hope that he at least might be able to influence Charlotte. But Prince William did not even try. He agreed with her. He hoped that she would come with him to Holland sometimes, but it would be quite unreasonable to make her come against her will.

The Prince Regent had lost. But he took his time to accept and admit it. It was not until 6 June that he went round to Warwick House, accompanied by 'the Great UP', and told Charlotte that her marriage contract would stipulate that she must not leave England against her will.

Next day Tsar Alexander of Russia and King Frederick of Prussia were welcomed into London by cheering crowds.

On his arrival at Dover, the Tsar had told the crowd on the dock, 'God be praised! I have set foot upon the land that has saved us all.' But it was only a courteous gesture. Just as the Prince Regent behaved as though he was personally responsible for every allied victory, the handsome and unusually liberal Tsar was rather more reasonably convinced that it was the Russians who had been the deciding force in the defeat of Napoleon.

The little British army had tied down enormous numbers of French soldiers in Spain. The Royal Navy had destroyed Napoleon's fleet. The British government had provided the subsidies that paid for Prussian and Austrian troops. But it was the Russians, their winter and the vastness of their country that had destroyed Napoleon's Grande Armée.

Tsar Alexander was now wary of the British. He harboured suspicions regarding their ambitions in Europe, and he was alarmed at the prospect of an overwhelming combination of the Dutch fleet and the Royal Navy. Since 1812 the British had been at war with the United States, and blockading British warships were at that very moment preventing Russian merchantmen from trading in New York harbour.

But the British government was also wary of the Tsar. He was not a reliable ally. After his initial defeats he had, like his father before him, changed sides, formed an alliance with Napoleon and declared war on Great Britain – two years later, when the Grand Duchess Catherine married Prince George of Oldenberg, some gossips said that she only did it to avoid being forced to marry Napoleon, who had just divorced Josephine.

In 1812, however, when Napoleon invaded Russia, suspecting correctly that the Tsar was thinking about changing sides again, the Russian ruler was left with no choice but to do what he was planning to do anyway.

Not for the last time, British and Russian allies were emerging from a terrible war in a mixed mood of gratitude and mistrust.

When the King of Prussia and the Tsar of Russia reached Carlton House, where they were due to stay, the King disliked the opulent furniture in his bedroom so much that he asked to be given a simple camp-bed, and the Tsar disliked the Prince Regent so much that he climbed into his Ambassador's coach and went round to the Pulteney Hotel to stay with his sister instead.

As he walked up the steps to the hotel door, the Tsar turned and raised his hat to acknowledge the cheers of the crowd. Londoners were to grow hoarse with cheering in the course of the next few weeks. Their capital contained all the great allied commanders, ex- cept Wellington, who was on duty in Paris, and they cheered every one of them wherever he went. Loudest of all, they cheered the 72-year-old Prussian Field Marshal Blücher, who was given the freedom of the city for doing more than anyone in central Europe to defeat the French army in the field. They cheered all the emperors and the kings. In the absence of the Emperor of Austria, who had stayed at home, they cheered his chancellor, Prince Metternich. They cheered the dozens of minor princes, even though they seldom knew who they were. They cheered Charlotte. They still cheered her mother. But they did not cheer the Prince Regent or the Queen. Indeed they sometimes spat at them. The people were still incensed at the ostracising of the Princess of Wales.

When all the sovereigns, princes, statesmen and commanders were received at court, the only members of the royal family who were – conspicuously – absent were the Princess of Wales and her daughter Princess Charlotte. Realising that this was a slight, the Tsar and his sister decided to go up to Connaught House and call on the Princess of Wales. But they were dissuaded by their Ambassador, who threatened to resign if they did – his wife was having an affair with Earl Grey at the time, and as a result he knew rather more than most people about the real nature of the Princess of Wales.

The Tsar and his sister did have a chance to see the Princess of Wales, however. It was on the evening when all the royal guests went to the opera. The Prince Regent sat in the royal box with the Tsar of Russia, the King of Prussia and the Grand Duchess Catherine, and the other princes sat in the boxes on their left. As they entered to the strains of the national anthem, they saw that the Princess of Wales was standing in the box opposite.

When the anthem was over, some of the young men in the stalls encouraged the audience to applaud the Princess of Wales. Her lady-in-waiting, Lady Charlotte Campbell, suggested that she should rise and acknowledge the applause with a curtsey.

'My dear', said the Princess, 'Punch's wife is nobody when Punch is present.'

She was sure that her husband would think that the applause was for him. And sure enough she was right. The Prince Regent stood up and bowed to the audience in acknowledgement.

At the end of the performance, the audience stood and applauded again as the Prince Regent and the other sovereigns left. But they were applauding his guests, not him. When they had all gone, the audience turned and directed much warmer applause to the box where the Princess of Wales was still standing. This time she acknowledged it with three smiling curtsies.

A few days later, however, at a breakfast party near Woolwich, she was seen sitting under a tree in the garden with a pot of strong beer on her knee. By the end of the party she was in a mood to be merry. She ordered all the doors in the house to be opened, grabbed a partner and set off at a gallop, calling to the other guests to follow her in flat-out procession through every room.

It was not regarded as seemly conduct for a member of the royal family. Some of the gentlemen present had been among those who led the applause at the opera. After seeing their reaction to the latest spectacle, one of the ladies, the Hon. Amelia Murray, reported that, in her opinion, they would not be so anxious to clap the Princess again.

On 10 June, while her father and most of his guests were at Ascot at the races, Charlotte signed her marriage contract and sent it round to Carlton House. In the evening she learned that her 'Slender Billy' had been made drunk at Ascot by Prince Paul of Wurtemberg and sent back to London like a day-tripper on top of a stagecoach. It was not the first time she had heard about her prince getting drunk – it was said that he got drunk on a visit back to Oxford – and it was not to be the last.

Two days later Charlotte attended the great banquet which her father gave for all his visitors at Carlton House. It was the only state occasion that she was allowed to attend. She had never seen anything like it. The house was full of young princes and officers. Next to most of these, her own Prince of Orange, who was a little bit drunk again, did not look like much of a catch.

By common consent, the handsomest of all was a tall, very dark young officer wearing the striking all-white uniform of the Russian heavy cavalry. When Charlotte noticed him he was at the other end of the crimson drawing room talking earnestly to a young lady.

According to one of the friends who were with her, Charlotte turned to them and 'observed how strange it was that the young lady did not seem more gratified by his attention'.

Charlotte did not get a chance to be introduced to this officer. But during the evening she was introduced to another, who was very charming, distinguished, almost as handsome and about ten years older than the hero in white. He was Prince Friedrich Wilhelm Heinrich August von Preussen, a nephew of Frederick the Great. In the course of the next month, with the giddy assistance of Cornelia Knight, this Prince was to be calling recklessly often at Warwick House.

CHAPTER ELEVEN

The Pulteney Hotel

———

ACCORDING TO CHARLOTTE'S uncle the Duke of Kent, Prince Friedrich Wilhelm Heinrich August was the only 'black sheep' in the Prussian royal family.

August, as he was known, was a good soldier. He fought with distinction at the battles of Auerstädt and Prenzlau, where he was wounded and captured. For a year after that he was a prisoner in France. But, like most high-ranking prisoners, he was given a certain amount of freedom in return for his promise not to attempt an escape. He was allowed to visit Madame de Staël, who was then holding court in the country at Coppet, and it was there that he met the famously beautiful Madame Récamier.

When she was only sixteen Juliette Récamier had been married to a banker who was forty-eight and probably impotent. For a dozen years her salon had been the most fashionable and cultured in Paris. But in 1806, when her husband lost all his money and could no longer afford to support her salon, she went to stay for a while with Madame de Staël.

In the following year Prince August came to call on her hostess. By then he was twenty-nine and Juliette Récamier was thirty. Inevitably, like almost every man who met her, he fell in love with her; to the surprise of everyone at Coppet, the notoriously cold-blooded beauty also fell in love with him. He was, she admitted, the only one of her many lovers who ever made her heart beat. They met often. When Prince August went back to Prussia, they exchanged letters. When the Prince proposed, Madame Récamier accepted. She would marry him if her husband would give her a divorce.

Jacques-Rose Récamier loved his wife so much that he was willing to let her go if it would make her happy, and he told her so in a letter so eloquent that even she was moved by it. She could not bring herself to abandon him in adversity. So it was Prince August's heart that was broken, not Monsieur Récamier's.

After that Prince August ceased to care. He was impetuous in battle and charmingly intemperate everywhere else. He became the kind of officer that old Blücher loved, and he commanded a brigade for him at the three-day battle of Leipzig. He was the lover of many mistresses, sometimes simultaneously, and he was the acknowledged father of several bastards. When he came to London in 1814 he brought with him two hard-earned reputations as a hero and a libertine.

Charlotte's head was turned by him, and so, unfortunately, was Cornelia Knight's. He was worldly, entertaining and confident. Within days he and Charlotte were exchanging presents, including rings. They promised to write to each other after August returned to Prussia, and Miss Knight agreed to act as their secret messenger.

For once the lady companion's common sense had deserted her. She may not have known much about Prince August's private life, but she did know that he was almost twice Charlotte's age, and that Charlotte was engaged to somebody else. And yet none of this seems to have mattered. To Miss Knight, this was much more the sort of prince who ought to be courting her beloved Princess.

Mercer, who must have known much more about the Prince, did

not agree with her. When she went round to Warwick House one day she was met in the hall by an excited 'Chevalier' and told that Charlotte was alone in her room with Prince August.

Mercer was horrified. She insisted that Miss Knight must go upstairs and sit with them or ask the Prince to leave. When she refused, Mercer went up and broke up the meeting herself.

Prince August had little to lose. He had a reputation for this sort of thing already. But Charlotte's reputation was impeccable, and it would have to stay that way if she ever wanted to be married. Even if she had not been engaged, the rumour that she was having secret assignations with a man like Prince August would have done at least as much damage as the story of her 'folly' with the little hussar.

But, despite the freedom that it promised, Charlotte's enthusiasm for her engagement was waning, and this was not just due to the attraction of Prince August, or the discovery that her betrothed was a callow, scruffy boy who could not even hold his liquor. Other forces were at work, trying to change her mind as well.

The more moderate Whigs, like Earl Grey and the Duke of Sussex, still had reservations about the cost of a close Dutch alliance, and they were still concerned that the Prince Regent had only been trying to get his daughter out of the country in order to induce his wife to leave as well. But the Radical Whigs, like Brougham and Whitbread, felt thwarted by the Regent's capitulation. They were still passionately opposed to the marriage.

The restriction imposed on Charlotte's visits to her mother and her mother's continuing exclusion from court were political weapons that the Radicals were loath to lose. Making indignant criticisms of both or either was still their best way of embarrassing the Regent and his government. But if Charlotte got married, they would be bound to lose one. As mistress of her own household, she would be entitled to receive anyone she pleased, including her mother. And if her mother went abroad, either because Charlotte had gone or else because she disapproved of the marriage, they would lose both.

Brougham was blunt. At a secret meeting, he warned Charlotte of what he saw as the consequences of marriage. Her mother would no longer have a good reason for staying in England, and her father might even bribe her to go. Once her mother was out of the country, she would no longer be a focus for popular support. Her father would be able to divorce her quietly without too much public opposition. If that happened, he would probably get married again, and if that happened, he might well have a son. Once there was a male heir, Charlotte could no longer look forward to being Queen of England. For the time being, he said, it was Charlotte's duty not to marry and stand by her mother.

So Charlotte had three reasons for avoiding marriage – the dismal prospect of Prince William himself; the hope that she might marry some other prince, preferably Prince August; and the duty to stand by her mother which, incidentally, would also protect her own position as heir presumptive.

Since Mercer was in London at the time, there is no written evidence of Charlotte's real motive, but the reason that she chose as an excuse was her duty to stay loyal to her mother.

On 16 June Charlotte had a meeting with William at Warwick House and told him that she could only marry him if he would accept that her mother would always be welcome in their home. When he said that he would never be allowed to agree to that, she told him that she could not marry him. The Hereditary Prince could not believe it. He asked her to think again and then left, offended and crestfallen.

Charlotte thought again and wrote to him that evening, with words, grammar and spelling that sounded more like the voice of Brougham than her own.

After reconsidering according to your wishes the conversation that passed between us this morning, I am still of the opinion that the duties and affection that naturally bind us to our respective countries render our marriage incompatible... From recent circumstances that have occurred I am fully convinced my interest is materially connected with that of my mother... After what has passed upon this subject this morning between us (which was much too conclusive to require further explanation) I must consider our engagement from this moment to be <u>totally and for ever at an end</u>. I leave the explanation of this affair to be made by you to the Prince...

She then ended with her sincere concern for causing him pain and asked him to accept her best wishes for his happiness.

Two days later she received a brief reply. 'I found the night before last your letter, and have lost no time to acquaint my family with its contents, but cannot comply with your wish by doing the same with regard to the Regent... Hoping that you shall never feel any cause to repent of the step you have now taken, I remain... etc.'

'Good English he writes', said Charlotte sarcastically.

Since Charlotte was the one who had broken off the engagement, it was reasonable to say that she was the one who should tell her father, but Charlotte thought it was cowardly. When she wrote to her father herself that day, she made out that it was the Prince who had broken off the engagement. 'He told me that our duties were divided, that our respective interests were in our different countries... Such an avowal was sufficient at once to prove to me Domestick happiness was out of the question.'

The Prince Regent received the news 'with astonishment, grief and concern'. When it got out, as it was bound to do, the Radical Whigs and the Princess of Wales were jubilant. But the Regent and his advisers bided their time. His imperial and royal guests were about to leave. Since they were all sympathetic to Charlotte, it would be wiser to let them go before starting any family rows.

❊

Charlotte and Cornelia Knight went round to the Pulteney Hotel to join the throng of others who had gone to say goodbye to the Tsar and his sister. When at last they reached the Grand Duchess Catherine's apartment, she led Charlotte into an anteroom and came out leaving her alone with the Tsar. Miss Knight insisted that this was improper and that she must join them. When she entered, the Tsar was trying in vain to make Charlotte reconsider her marriage. The Hereditary Prince of Orange was in the building. She had only to find him and tell him that she had changed her mind. He went up to a newspaper lying on a table and pointed at a paragraph as he spoke. She was 'giving up an excellent marriage, one essential to the interests of her country, and all to be praised by a Mr Whitbread'.

The Tsar accepted defeat and took his leave. Charlotte came out of the anteroom agitated. If she left now she was bound to meet the Hereditary Prince in the waiting room or on the stairs or in the hall. The Grand Duchess led her to a small door, opened it and pointed to the back stairs. She kissed Princess Charlotte, and then, to the great delight of the lady companion, she kissed Cornelia Knight.

Charlotte and Miss Knight beat their undignified retreat down the back stairs, which led into a little hall beside the main hall. Several people had come into it to avoid the crush in the main hall, and one of them, at the foot of the stairs with his back to them, was a tall, dark, handsome officer wearing the all-white uniform of the Russian heavy cavalry.

The officer turned. He was not more than twenty-four years old, but his badges signified that he was already a Lieutenant-General. He asked if he could help the ladies. Miss Knight explained that this was the Princess Charlotte of Wales and that they would be grateful if he would see them to her carriage.

The officer escorted the ladies through the throng, found the carriage and handed them into it.

Charlotte thanked him and asked his name.

When she learned he was a prince, she scolded him for not having called on her like most of the other princes.

The Prince begged her forgiveness and asked to be allowed to make up for his omission.

Charlotte consented.

The carriage drove away.

The Prince walked back up the steps to the hotel.

He was the General Officer Commanding the Heavy Cavalry of the Tsar, Prince Leopold of Saxe-Coburg-Saalfeld.

Chapter Twelve

The Officer at the Foot of the Stairs

———❧———

PRINCE LEOPOLD GEORGE Christian Frederick, the youngest child of Duke Francis of Saxe-Coburg-Saalfeld, was born on 16 December 1790. His family was descended from the eleventh-century Margraves of Meissen and Lausitz, but in the seven hundred years since then few of his ancestors had made a mark on the pages of European history. The most distinguished was Frederick the Wise, who, at the beginning of the sixteenth century, refused the throne of the Holy Roman Empire, supported Martin Luther and converted all his subjects to Protestantism. Frederick's great-grandson, John William, was one of the many suitors who failed to marry Queen Elizabeth of England; another ancestor, Ernest the Pious, served in the army of Gustavus Adolphus and was one of the first rulers to establish free schools for his subjects.

Like most of the younger sons of the many German rulers, Leopold was educated to make his own way in the world as a soldier or a diplomat. He learned Christian ethics, Latin, Russian, French and English. He was taught to draw, to play the piano, to ride and to fence. But he was also taught to be ambitious – and for that there were plenty of role models in his family. Unlike their ancestors, the latest generations of the House of Coburg were hungry for power, position and wealth.

During the first few years of Leopold's life his uncle Frederick was commanding an Austrian army in the Netherlands. His eldest brother Ernest, who succeeded their father as Duke, became a general in the Russian army and married an eccentric German heiress, who added the neighbouring estates of Gotha to Coburg and Saalfeld. His other brother, Ferdinand, served in the Austrian army and married an even richer Hungarian princess.

The only one of his four sisters who married for love was Sophia, the eldest. Her husband was one of the many refugees who fled to Germany from France on the outbreak of the Revolution. He was only a count, but he was a rich count who had managed to bring most of his money with him, and he was a good friend to Leopold.

The other sisters married for position. Antoinette married Duke Alexander of Wurtemberg; Victoria married Prince Emich Charles of Leningen; and Julia did best of all. She married the brother of the Tsar, the Grand Duke Constantine.

With such a sister, it was not difficult for a beautiful boy to find favour and patronage at the Russian court. Leopold was enlisted as a cadet in the Imperial Guard when he was only five, soon after his sister's wedding. In the following year he was given the honorary commission of captain. Next year he was made a colonel.

After that Julie grew tired of her husband's cruelty and went home to Coburg. But Leopold remained a favourite with the Grand Duke and the Tsar. On 15 May 1803, when he was still only twelve, they made him a general.

Two years later, when Napoleon advanced against the armies of Austria and Russia, intrepid, fourteen-year-old Leopold set out to turn his honorary commission into a real one. But he arrived too late. Two days after he reached the Russian headquarters, news came that the allies had been crushed at Austerlitz.

Leopold went home. In the following year, when Napoleon went to war with Prussia, Coburg was overrun and plundered by the French. There was no resistance. Leopold's father, the Duke, was already on his deathbed; his eldest brother, the heir, who had gone to join the Prussian army, was also in bed, immobilised by typhoid fever.

The Duke died. The French took over the government of his duchy and incorporated it into the Confederation of the Rhine. Coburg became part of the French Empire.

Since the new Duke was still in bed a hundred and fifty miles away, his formidable mother took up his cause. She demanded an audience with Napoleon. When he refused, she turned to the Tsar, who was then in the process of changing sides and was about to become Napoleon's ally. The Tsar agreed to help. One of the terms of the treaty that he signed with Napoleon at Tilsit, on 7 July 1807, was that Coburg, while remaining part of the Confederation, was to be restored to the rule of young Duke Ernest.

As soon as he recovered from his fever, Ernest went to thank Napoleon at his headquarters in Dresden. He was received warmly. The Emperor even promised to increase the size of his duchy by adding a large part of Bayreuth to it. But within weeks of his homecoming, Ernest was on the edge of bankruptcy. Even with the additional income from Gotha, which he had acquired through his wife, his ruined estates in Coburg and Saalfeld were incapable of providing enough revenue to pay for all the soldiers that Napoleon was demanding for his army. So Ernest decided to follow the Emperor to Paris and remind him of his promise and, knowing that good looks and charm were advantages diplomatically as well as socially, he took his brother Leopold with him.

They arrived in Paris on 14 October. Napoleon was not there. The Palace of the Tuileries was occupied by no one but guards and servants. While they waited, however, the brothers were received out at Malmaison by the Empress Josephine, and it was there that Leopold was introduced to her beautiful daughter Hortense.

Leopold was then two months short of his seventeenth birthday, and Hortense was twenty-four. She was married to Napoleon's brother Louis, the King of Holland, but she had left him and come back to live with her mother, and she was still in mourning for a baby son who had died suddenly five months earlier. Over the next few days, the unhappy Queen of Holland consoled herself by seducing the handsome Prince from Coburg.

Meanwhile Ernest had met a famous Greek beauty, Pauline Panam. For almost six months, Ernest and Leopold stayed in Paris with nothing to do but enjoy the company of Pauline and Hortense.

At last, in March 1808, the French Emperor returned to his capital. Before setting out again for Spain, he granted a brief audience to the brothers from Coburg. It was not a success. Napoleon remembered his promise to Ernest but did nothing to fulfil it, and when Leopold asked to be taken onto his staff as an aide-de-camp, he declined to decide one way or the other. There were, however, dozens of young princes looking for jobs on the Emperor's staff in 1808, and at least Leopold was one of the few who left an impression on him. In Napoleon's opinion, Prince Leopold was the handsomest man who ever set foot in the Tuileries.

In terms of position and worldly wealth, the brothers left Paris empty-handed. But they were both the richer in experience, and Ernest had something to show for it as well. He was accompanied by Pauline Panam, 'la belle Greque'. To avoid any chance of scandal, she travelled dressed as a man. When they reached the city of Coburg, she was set up discreetly on a farm nearby, where, a few months later, she gave birth to a child.

※

In October Leopold went to Erfurt where Napoleon, the Tsar and many of the leading rulers in the Confederation of the Rhine had assembled for a conference. In reality it was more of a celebration than a conference. There were more balls, banquets and parades than meetings. But amid these Leopold managed to obtain an audience with the Emperor, at which he repeated his brother's request for more land and his own for a position on the imperial staff. The answer to the former was more encouraging and more specific than before. Napoleon agreed to add parts of Bayreuth and Bamberg to Coburg. But the answer to the latter was still non-committal.

In later life Leopold always denied that he had asked for a position. He said that it was Napoleon who offered him a job and that he had turned it down. But Napoleon told a different story, and Napoleon was the one who had no reason to disguise the truth. During his exile on St Helena, he told the Comte de las Cases, 'This Prince Leopold might have been my aide-de-camp; he begged it of me; I don't know what prevented his appointment. It is very lucky for him he did not succeed.'

In 1808 Leopold could not have felt that he was doing anything dishonourable or disloyal. His homeland was part of the French Empire, and he had been granted an honorary commission by the Tsar, who was then Napoleon's ally. Like so many other princes, he simply sought advancement in the entourage of his new commander. After Napoleon's defeat, however, it was unlikely that others would see it that way. To have asked for such a job would not have looked good in England, and to have succeeded in obtaining it would have made Leopold ineligible for almost all the honours and offices that were subsequently offered to him.

Leopold left Erfurt and went back to Coburg. Four years later Napoleon summoned the princes of the German Confederation to Dresden. He was preparing to invade Russia. Leopold, now twenty-one years old, decided not to attend. Technically his loyalties were divided. He was a citizen in Napoleon's empire, but he was an officer in the Tsar's army. Yet while his conscience was telling him his loyalties lay with Russia, his common sense was telling him to wait and see what happened.

Common sense prevailed. Leopold went to Italy and waited. The French army reached Moscow and then retreated from its ruins. By the time it crossed the border, it had been almost annihilated by the Russian winter and relentless Cossacks.

On 28 February 1813, when the Russian and Prussian leaders met at Kalish to form an alliance against Napoleon, Leopold was there. When he reported for duty, he was given the real rank of colonel and attached to the staff of the Imperial Guard.

In his first battle, the allies' defeat at Lutzen, Leopold commanded a brigade of cavalry. It may still have been an honorary command, with other officers making the decisions, but in the Russian army, which was notorious in those days for the ineptitude of its officers, it was not difficult for an able man to get noticed. Three weeks later, at Bautzen, Leopold took charge of the brigade himself. He led it out in front of the advancing French and covered the allied retreat into Silesia.

After that Leopold was a cavalry commander. He played a key role in the victory at Kulm, where he was decorated in the field with the Cross of St George. He led a charge at the great battle of Leipzig and was decorated again, this time with the Cross of Maria Theresa. At the end of the campaign, he led the Russian heavy cavalry on its westward advance from Switzerland towards Paris, engaging the enemy at Brienne, Fere-Champenoise and Bellville.

On 31 March 1814, riding at the head of his cuirassiers, and wearing the well-earned insignia of a Lieutenant-General, Leopold escorted the Tsar of Russia and the King of Prussia into the French capital.

❋

While he was in Paris, Leopold renewed his friendship with Hortense and visited her frequently in her blue boudoir on the Rue Cerutti. On 25 April he wrote to his sister Sophia: 'The Tsar is going to

England, and I am very tempted to make the journey, because there will be a great many festivities. But it would cost too much.'

By then, however, the Tsar had been receiving letters from his sister in London. The proposed marriage between England and Holland was not in Russia's best interest, but it was clear that England's Princess Charlotte was more interested in marriage than in her future husband. If she could be introduced to a prince who was handsome, charming and successful, she might at least be induced to think twice about the Hereditary Prince of Orange.

The next time Leopold sat down to write to his favourite sister his plans had changed. The Tsar was taking him in his entourage to London.

Leopold borrowed a carriage from Sophia's husband, and in return he lent him the castle in Austria which had just been given to him by the grateful Emperor. He visited the best tailors in Paris. He spent so much that when he reached crowded London the only lodgings he could afford were two rooms on the second floor of number 21 Marylebone High Street, which he rented from Mr Hole, who ran a greengrocer's shop on the ground floor. The simple lodgings were not without advantages, however. When he was not in attendance on the Tsar or out and about in London society, Leopold spent most of his time with Mr Hole's young housemaid, who was overwhelmed by the handsome Prince and adored the way his eyelids drooped slightly when he bowed.

In the light of all this, it may not have been a coincidence that Leopold was waiting at the foot of the back stairs when Charlotte left the Grand Duchess's apartments after saying goodbye to her; it may be that the Tsar was only testing her when he asked her to make peace with the young Prince of Orange. Certainly his dismissive sneer at 'a Mister Whitbread' was disingenuous. The liberal Tsar was in sympathy with the Whigs. He had received Samuel Whitbread at the Pulteney Hotel; and he had angered the Regent by greeting him warmly at a reception.

A few days after the Tsar left London, Leopold wrote significantly to his eldest brother:

> The Tsar has given me permission to stay here as long as it suits me. I only decided to do so after much hesitation, and after certain very singular events made me glimpse the possibility, even the probability, of realising the project we spoke of in Paris. My chances are, alas, very poor, because of the father's opposition, and he will never give his consent. But I have resolved to go on to the end, and only to leave when all my hopes have been destroyed...

By then Leopold had visited Charlotte. He left a state concert before it ended and went round to Warwick House wearing his full dress uniform. While he was there, Mercer arrived. She was delighted by the surprise. She already knew the Prince and she approved of him. For her, this was much more the sort of prince who ought to be courting the future Queen of England.

After that, more often than not, when Charlotte and Miss Knight took the air in Hyde Park, Leopold just happened to be there as well. Each time the Princess acknowledged him with a nod, and each time, in response, the Prince trotted up to her carriage and rode beside her for a while.

During the last ten days of June and the first ten of July, 'the Great UP' called at Warwick House at least twice to warn Charlotte that, if she did not submit to her father and agree to marry the Hereditary Prince of Orange, 'arrangements would be made by no means agreeable to her inclinations'. But Charlotte was having too good a time to take notice. She was being courted by two handsome suitors, each one supported, encouraged and championed by one of her two closest confidantes. Prince August of Prussia was still Cornelia Knight's candidate, and Prince Leopold of Saxe-Coburg was now Mercer Elphinstone's.

Chapter Thirteen

'I Have Run Off'

———

J UST BEFORE 5 p.m. on the evening of Monday, 11 July 1814, Cornelia Knight walked over from Warwick House for a meeting with the Prince Regent at Carlton House. Princess Charlotte had been summoned as well, but she had stayed behind, claiming that a sore knee prevented her from walking.

Miss Knight was anxious, the more so for being left to face the Regent on her own. A few days earlier her friend Lady Rolle had warned her that the Prince was planning changes, and had reassured her that, if she suddenly needed somewhere to stay, she would always be welcome at the Rolles' London house. Since then she had learned that the Duchess of Leeds had been asked to resign. Naturally the lady companion now feared for her own position as well.

The Regent was 'very cold, very bitter, and very silent'. He had heard that a German prince had been paying court to his daughter.

Miss Knight assured him that Prince Leopold of Saxe-Coburg was an honourable man. He had called only once at Warwick House and had behaved impeccably, and both she and the Duchess had been present throughout his visit.

The Regent did not disagree. He knew that Prince Leopold had behaved entirely properly. He had just received a long letter from the young Prince assuring him that his intentions were honourable and that he had only gone to Warwick House at the invitation of the Princess. The Prince about whom he complained was Prince August of Prussia.

When Miss Knight had delivered a similar but slightly less honest defence of Prince August, the Regent dismissed her and warned that, if his daughter did not come next day to explain herself, he would go to her.

Back at Warwick House, where Mercer was waiting with Charlotte, Miss Knight reported all that had been said. Charlotte and Mercer were disappointed. They had hoped that Prince Leopold was romantic enough to keep his courting a secret, and Miss Knight was dismayed to have discovered that Prince August's courting was even less of a secret.

Next day, after Mercer had returned from spending the night at her own house, Charlotte sent a note asking her father to come to her. Eventually he came, at six in the evening, accompanied by the 'Bish-UP' of Salisbury.

While the Bishop waited downstairs, the Regent went up and saw Charlotte alone behind closed doors in the drawing room. Miss Knight waited in the anteroom where she and the Regent had once waited with the door open. After three quarters of an hour, he came out and summoned the Bishop.

A quarter of an hour after that Charlotte came out, almost hysterical. Her father had now summoned Miss Knight. They had only 'one instant' to talk.

Miss Knight followed the Princess into her dressing room. Her father, she said, had decided to dismiss everyone. All the servants were to go, and Miss Knight would be required to leave immediately. New ladies were waiting to take over from her. As soon as possible, within a few days, Charlotte was to be sent to

Windsor, not to Lower Lodge, but to Cranbourne Lodge, in the middle of the forest, where she was to be kept in isolation. No one would be allowed to visit her but the Queen, and even she would only come once a week.

The Princess fell on her knees. 'God Almighty grant me patience!'

Cornelia Knight began to comfort her, but Charlotte insisted that she must go to the Regent before he became angrier.

The admiral's daughter went into the drawing room and stood defiantly in front of the Regent and his pompous Bishop. He told her what Charlotte had told her already. He asked her to leave at once since he needed her room for the new ladies. When she asked what she had done to offend, he refused to give a reason and said simply that he had 'a right to make any changes he pleased'.

When she came out of the drawing room Miss Knight was met by Mercer and Mrs Louis, who was weeping. The Princess had run away. Mrs Louis thought she might have gone to Carlton House, but Mercer had heard her say she was going to her mother.

Mercer and Miss Knight went in to tell the Regent together. To their surprise, he seemed rather pleased. He said, Miss Knight wrote later, that 'he was glad that everybody would now see what she was, and that it would be known on the Continent, and no one would marry her'.

Meanwhile, in Pall Mall, Mr Collins, an architect, was looking out of the window above his uncle's print shop when he saw a frantic young lady who was obviously in great distress. He went down and asked if he could help her. She asked him to call her a hackney-coach. He found one, handed her into it and watched as it drove away westward and then turned north-west.

Inside the coach the passenger instructed the driver, Mr Higgins, to take her to Oxford Street. When they reached it she directed him to Connaught House, where she told the servant who opened the door to give her driver an extravagant three guineas. It was only then, when he saw the house and the low bow of the servant, that Mr Higgins realised who his passenger had been.

The Princess of Wales had gone to dine in Blackheath. Charlotte sent a groom to gallop after her and bring her home as fast as possible. She ordered dinner, and then she gave quickly-scribbled notes to two of her mother's coachmen and sent them off to find and bring back Brougham and her Whig uncle, the Duke of Sussex. Each note began with the same words: 'I have run off.'

The groom caught up with Charlotte's mother on the road. By 9 a.m. she was back in her own house and sitting down to dinner with Henry Brougham and her daughter. Brougham was not hungry, he had already dined, and he was exhausted. He had been up all the previous night working on a case. When Charlotte suggested that he could at least carve, he told her that the only dish he felt fit to carve was the soup.

Charlotte recounted all that had happened and said that she had run away because she could take no more of her father's bullying. Her plan now was to stand by her mother and live with her if she could. But it was a plan that her mother met with somewhat less enthusiasm than might have been expected. Unknown to Charlotte her father had offered to increase her mother's allowance to £50,000 a year, and now that Europe was at peace again, her mother was contemplating exactly what her father had hoped – a little bit of foreign travel.

The party was upstairs in the drawing room when Mercer arrived accompanied by 'the Great UP'. After Charlotte's flight, when the Prince Regent went off to join a card party at the Duke of York's apartments, Mercer and the Bishop had agreed to go up to Connaught House and try to persuade Charlotte to come home, and Cornelia Knight had refused to come with them because she could no longer bring herself to set foot in a house that belonged to the Princess of Wales.

Mercer was invited up to the drawing room, while the Bishop

was shown into the dining room. It was a pattern of precedence that was to be maintained throughout the night. Partisans of the Princess were brought straight upstairs: representatives of the Regent were at best shown into the dining room and in most cases not even admitted to the house.

The Bishop did not have to wait too long, however. He was soon sent back to find the Regent with a note from Charlotte, in which she promised to return to Warwick House provided she was allowed to see Mercer as often as she wished, and provided Miss Knight and Mrs Louis were allowed to remain members of her household.

He had not been long gone when a series of coaches and carriages arrived carrying the Lord Chancellor, the Lord Chief Justice and the other law officers, advisers and privy councillors who had been summoned and sent out by the Regent. To Brougham's much amused embarrassment, Charlotte merrily instructed the servants to tell them all to wait in their carriages.

Then Cornelia Knight arrived. As soon as Mercer and the Bishop had left Warwick House she had become so anxious about Charlotte that she changed her mind. She would have come after them then and there if she could. She had sent a note to Lady Salisbury explaining the emergency and asking if she could borrow her carriage. But the carriage had not been available until after it had dropped Lady Salisbury at the opera house.

In her memoir, Cornelia Knight wrote that once she was in the drawing room she gave Charlotte her royal seal, a key and a letter that had arrived after her departure. But she did not say who it was from.

The next to come was the Duke of Sussex. He had been dining with friends when Charlotte's cry for help arrived. It was so illegible that he had stuffed it in his pocket. It had taken a second note from Brougham to bring him.

Outside in the street, accepting that they were never going to be admitted, the law officers, advisers and privy councillors turned their carriages and drove away. Upstairs in the drawing room the Duke of Sussex asked Brougham whether it would be lawful to resist if the Regent tried to take Charlotte away by force.

Brougham shook his head. 'It would not', he said.

The Duke turned to Charlotte. 'Then my dear, you hear what the law is. I can only advise you to return with as much speed and as little noise as possible.'

But Charlotte was not yet ready to take that sort of advice, even though Mercer and her mother agreed with it. She was still waiting for the Bishop to come back with her father's answer to her note – and Miss Knight was already tired of waiting. She would go down to Carlton House and see what was happening, and if possible she would confront the Regent. Since Lady Salisbury's carriage had been sent back to the opera house, she went in one of the carriages from Connaught House.

When the impetuous 'Chevalier' reached Carlton House she found that all the eminent lawyers who had been waiting for Charlotte outside Connaught House were now waiting for the Regent in his drawing room. He was still playing cards, they said. But they knew that the Bishop had reached him, and that the Bishop was now on his way back to Connaught House.

Suspecting that Charlotte might want to spend the night with her mother, Miss Knight went over to Warwick House and asked Mrs Louis to pack a bag with Charlotte's nightdress and anything else she might need. When it was done, they set off together in the carriage.

By the time they reached Connaught House the Bishop had delivered the Regent's answer. Charlotte could go on seeing Mercer, but that was all. It was not enough. The friendly pleading and the obstinacy continued.

Some time between two and three in the morning the Duke of York arrived. He had always been a good friend to Charlotte, and as a Royal Duke he deserved to be received with respect, but on this occasion he was the Regent's representative. He was shown into the dining room.

If the party upstairs had known that he was carrying a warrant empowering him to take the Princess home by force if necessary, they might have been a bit more cautious. Nevertheless the Princess of Wales did go down to talk to him. When she came back she reported that the Duke had been sent from his own card party to bring Charlotte back to Carlton House. He had not mentioned the warrant.

The night went on. Everybody pleaded. Charlotte, her eyes red with tears, still insisted that she would not go.

At last, shortly after dawn, Brougham led Charlotte to the window and showed her Hyde Park in the early sunlight. There was to be a by-election that morning. 'In a few hours', he said, 'all the streets and the park, now empty, will be crowded with tens of thousands. I have only to take you to that window and tell them your grievances, and they will all rise in your behalf.'

'And why should they not?' said Charlotte.

Brougham replied:

The commotion will be excessive; Carlton House will be attacked – perhaps pulled down; the soldiers will be ordered out; blood will be shed; and if your Royal Highness were to live a hundred years, it never would be forgotten that your running away from your father's house was the cause of the mischief: and you may depend upon it, such is the English people's horror of bloodshed, you never would get over it.

Brougham had won again. The tearful Princess submitted. She would go back with the Duke of York to Carlton House. But she was a princess, and as such she insisted that she must be taken back in a royal coach. And while she waited for that coach to come she asked Brougham to write a short statement to the effect that she was determined never to marry the Prince of Orange, and that 'if ever there should be an announcement of such a match, it must be understood to be without her consent and against her will'. When it was written, she asked for six copies to be made, signed all of them and gave one to each person present.

Brougham was deeply impressed. 'I had no idea of her having so much good in her', he said.

The carriage came. While everyone else went downstairs to see the Princess off, Cornelia Knight stayed in the drawing room. By her own admission she was too miserable to go.

Charlotte took the Duke of York's hand and climbed into the carriage. The Duke stepped in and sat beside her. Her mother came forward. The Princess, she said, must be accompanied by her maid. The Duke refused. Charlotte insisted. Mrs Louis climbed in and sat shyly opposite the Duke and the Princess.

They drove down Park Lane, along Birdcage Walk and up the Mall to Carlton House. It had been a long night. But the Prince Regent's cruelty knew no bounds. The Princess and her maid were kept waiting in the courtyard for half an hour before they were admitted into the house.

Charlotte's father, before self-indulgence destroyed his figure, dressed as Colonel of the 10th Light Dragoons.

Below: Charlotte: an idealised portrait of the lonely Princess.

Left: Charlotte's mother in the wedding dress chosen for her by the Queen.

Charlotte, no longer a tomboy.

Leopold in Russian uniform.

Claremont, the house where Charlotte and Leopold lived for most of their
short married life.

Right: Charlotte's closest friend and confidante, the beautiful heiress Mercer Elphinstone.

Charlotte's lady companion and champion, Cornelia Knight, 'the Chevalier'.

The opulent Crimson Drawing Room at Carlton House, where Charlotte and Leopold were married.

Charlotte in a traditional Russian costume, a present from the Grand Duchess Catherine.

Charlotte wearing the diamond bracelet that her husband gave her as a wedding present.

The miniature of himself that Leopold gave to Charlotte.

The Tsar and the Grand Duchess Catherine on the balcony of the Pulteney Hotel.

Brilliant, cynical Henry Brougham, who manipulated public support for Charlotte and her mother in his own political interest.

Queen Hortense, daughter of the Empress Josephine, mother of the Emperor Napoleon III and mistress of Prince Leopold and Count Flahault.

Madame Récamier, the famous French beauty who broke Prince August's heart.

A cartoonist's representation of the Regent introducing the penniless German princeling to his daughter.

'Slender Billy', the Hereditary Prince of Orange. Leopold, he lamented, had taken 'his wife and his kingdom'.

Prince August, 'the only black sheep in the Prussian royal family'. A portrait of Madame Récamier hangs on the wall behind him.

Leopold wearing the moustache he grew to please Charlotte.

To BE, OR, NOT TO BE!

How Charlotte's father's coronation might have looked if her mother had been allowed to attend.

Leopold resplendent in the robes of a Knight of the Garter, which he wore to stunning effect at his father-in-law's coronation.

A ROUGH PASSAGE TO BELGIUM.

Overleaf:
The Regent and his mother, assisted by the Lord Chancellor, scrub up the verminous foreign Prince to make him fit for Charlotte.

The apprehensive Prince sets sail for his precarious new kingdom.

Chapter Fourteen

State Prisoner

On 15 July 1814 the Duke of Sussex wrote to the Prime Minister asking why Princess Charlotte of Wales was being held as a 'state prisoner' and demanding to be allowed to visit her.

He knew about Charlotte's condition because he had received a letter from her. It had been written on stolen paper with a pencil dipped in milk, and it had been delivered by a secret postal service that began with the French master, Mr Sterkey, and then ran on through Cornelia Knight and Mercer Elphinstone.

For all that she was living in the comfort of Carlton House, Charlotte was indeed a prisoner. The warders were the Dowager Countess of Ilchester, the Dowager Countess of Rosslyn, her two nieces, the Misses Coates, and one of Charlotte's former sub-governesses, Mrs Campbell, who, being a Tory, was now restored to favour with the Regent. There was always at least one of them watching her. Even at night one of them slept in her room, or else in the room beside it with the door open.

The only consolation was that loyal Mrs Louis had been allowed to stay on. But even she was as much of a prisoner as her Princess.

At night she was required to sleep on a sofa in Charlotte's room. By day, whatever she was doing, she was always accompanied by two of the Regent's own servants, one watching her and one guarding the door. When she went across to Warwick House to collect some of Charlotte's clothes, Lady Ilchester herself went with her and told her 'there must be no talking or messages'.

The only contact with the outside world lay through Mr Sterkey, Miss Knight and Mercer. Mercer did all that she dared to represent Charlotte's interests. She was in close touch with Brougham, Earl Grey and the Duke of Sussex – and she was in touch with Prince Leopold.

Leopold wrote to Mercer on 17 July, and next day they met. He was anxious about Charlotte and he was eager to see her. But Mercer held out no hope for him. As she told him in her reply to his note, Charlotte had been so offended by his letter to her father that it had 'put an end to all possibility of a happier future'.

If Charlotte really was offended that much, it can only have been because her father showed her the letter, or else because the naive old Bishop, who certainly did see it, described the contents to her in detail.

The letter was much more than the simple self-justification that the Regent described to Miss Knight. It was a blunt declaration of intent, combined with fawning flattery and not-too-subtle personal propaganda.

Leopold began by saying that he had only visited the Princess because she had invited him to do so. But he felt now that he might have offended her father by not asking his permission first, and that this was probably the reason for the coldness with which His Royal Highness had received him at a subsequent audience. Nevertheless he still had the confidence to assure the Regent that his intentions were serious, and to insist that, at a more appropriate time, they would be worthy of consideration.

'Your Royal Highness', he wrote, 'who knows human nature so

thoroughly, and judges it so wisely, will be too kind to blame me for the desire, but I beg you to be sure that, with a character so cool and steady as mine, I would not dream of making definite suggestions at the present moment.'

It looked as though Leopold was courting her father not Charlotte, and his letter was enough to make August the favourite. Dashing, worldly, carefree August was the one who had been brave enough to write directly, and secretly, to Charlotte; and his letters were apparently so affectionate and romantic that it was too dangerous to do anything but burn them as soon as they had been read.

But for the time being there was little that Leopold could have done anyway. On the day after his meeting with Mercer, Charlotte, her ladies and Mrs Louis were moved down to Windsor, to Cranbourne Lodge, and soon afterwards he received news that Prince Emich Charles of Leningen had died. By the end of the month he was in Bavaria comforting his widowed sister Victoria.

On her arrival at Cranbourne Lodge, Charlotte was alarmed to discover that Lady Ilchester was no longer her 'chief warder'. She and the other ladies were now under the direction of a male 'governor', a seventy-year-old retired general called Thomas Garth. But, to her relief, Charlotte soon formed a good impression of both the General and her new home. The General, she told Mercer, was 'very good hearted', even though he was 'very vulgar in his conversation and language'; the lodge, despite its isolation, was 'very cheerful' and 'far superior to the Lower Lodge'.

Next day the Duke of Sussex, who had received no answer to his letter to the Prime Minister, stood up in the House of Lords and asked him five very well informed questions: was the Princess Charlotte still allowed to receive visits from friends; was she still allowed what he described as 'the free exercise of her pen'; was she, as he put it, 'in the same state of liberty as a person not in confinement would be in'; had her doctors recommended a holiday by the sea, and if so would she be allowed to take one; and finally, now that she had reached the age at which she was constitutionally entitled to ascend the throne and rule without a regent, were there any plans to provide her with her own appropriate establishment?

Lord Liverpool declined to answer, on the grounds that to do so would be to accept the 'disagreeable' and 'unnecessary' implication of the questions.

The Duke was not satisfied. In response, he told their Lordships that he planned to call for a full debate and bring in a motion of censure against the government. But during the next few days he learned from the newspapers that Charlotte had been seen out riding with the General at Windsor, and Earl Grey persuaded him that public arguments were never the best way of resolving private royal quarrels.

The Duke withdrew his motion. The only outcome was that the Regent summoned him to Carlton House, rebuked him loudly, in language that would have shocked even General Garth, and then dismissed him like a servant and never spoke to him again.

※

In her isolation at Cranbourne Lodge Charlotte was at least allowed to see newspapers. She read that the motion had been withdrawn. The week went by. The sense of being watched was oppressive. The loneliness without the company of Miss Knight or any hope of being allowed to see Mercer was dispiriting.

Then her father appeared, accompanied by the 'Bish-UP', and told her with undisguised pleasure that her mother was planning to leave for an extended tour of the Continent. Charlotte would, of course, be allowed to go up to London to say goodbye.

Charlotte's mother had always been less supportive than Charlotte had hoped, and more of a liability than Charlotte was prepared to recognise. But her planned departure was as much of a blow to Charlotte as it was to Brougham, and the way in which she said farewell was very painful. When Charlotte went to Connaught House, she faced the truth for the first time. Her mother did not really care for her. The Princess of Wales was so excited about her impending adventure that she could not even bring herself to pretend. Her manner was 'indifferent'.

'I feel so hurt at <u>that</u> being a <u>leave-taking</u>', Charlotte wrote to Mercer, 'for God knows how long, or <u>what events</u> may occur before we meet again, or if ever she will return.'

The Royal Navy laid on the one warship that was accustomed to carrying important ladies. On 9 August the Princess of Wales boarded HMS *Jason* off Lancing and sailed south for France. Charlotte never saw her again.

For the rest of that month the principal preoccupation at the isolation lodge was the holiday that the Duke of Sussex mentioned in his questions to the Prime Minister. Charlotte, as the Duke knew, was longing for a holiday by the sea, and her doctors were all in favour of it. She really did have a sore, swollen knee, which was now so bad that they told her to stop riding, and since her arrival at Cranbourne Lodge she had been displaying symptoms of depression. The sea air, in their view, would be ideal for both. But, to everybody's exasperation, the Prince Regent prevaricated. As Earl Grey put it in one of his letters to Mercer, 'All the best season will be wasted before she gets to the sea-side.'

Charlotte wanted to take Mercer with her, but the Regent said no. He claimed that Mercer's father would not allow it. Lord Keith, he said, did not want his daughter to spend too much time in isolation with Charlotte, where there would be no chance of her meeting a suitable husband.

Charlotte wanted to go to fashionable Brighton, but the Regent said no to that as well. He wanted Brighton to himself. Eventually he asked the Queen if they could borrow Gloucester Lodge, a house that she and the King owned far away in Dorset, in no longer quite so fashionable Weymouth. The Queen took her time and then said yes, reluctantly. And so, at last, with September approaching, Weymouth was chosen as the setting for Charlotte's seaside holiday.

Shortly before she left, Charlotte went to a musical evening at Windsor Castle. When the music was over, one of her aunts, Princess Mary, took her aside and expressed genuine concern for her future. 'I see no chance for you of comfort', she said, 'and certainly not at present as things are, without your marrying'.

As she often did when marriage was mentioned, Charlotte threw in a red herring. She knew that everyone in the royal family disapproved of the recent marriage between her uncle the Duke of Cumberland and a widowed daughter of the Duke of Mecklenburg-Strelitz, Princess Frederica, who had once jilted his brother the Duke of Cambridge. So Charlotte suggested that she might marry Prince Charles of Mecklenburg-Strelitz.

'Oh, God, no', said Princess Mary, and then added, 'I would be the last now to recommend or to wish for anyone in particular.'

Charlotte then decided to ask her aunt about someone whom she genuinely regarded as a candidate.

She knew that there was no point in mentioning Prince August. Everyone in the royal family was aware that he had been paying court to Charlotte and they all disapproved of him. The well-meaning Duchess of York had even tried to put her off him by warning her that he liked ladies excessively and that his breath smelt. But the first criticism was one of the attributes that made him so dangerously attractive, and the second, if true, was clearly something that Charlotte and a great many other ladies were prepared to overlook.

August was still the favourite. He had just left London and, like Leopold, was on his way to Vienna. Most of the European rulers and their retinues were assembling there for the congress that everybody hoped would bring lasting peace. But Charlotte fully expected to stay in touch with August while he was away, not only through Miss Knight, but now through Mercer as well.

Nevertheless, although August was still the favourite, Leopold was not as much out of favour as Mercer had made out. Charlotte asked her aunt what she thought of him.

Princess Mary blushed noticeably. 'From what I saw of him, he was very good looking', she said. 'A very gentlemanlike young man.'

'I don't like him', said Charlotte, 'for he does not suit my taste'.

Princess Mary thought for a moment and then said, 'You don't... don't.'

The enigmatic answer, combined with the blush, convinced Charlotte that her aunt was being as deceptive as she was.

A few days later she screwed up the courage to ask another aunt directly whether her Aunt Mary was in favour of Prince Leopold or not. Princess Sophia honestly did not know, but she did know that the Duchess of York supported him. Leopold, she said, was 'the greatest possible favourite' with the Duchess of York. As for her own opinion, Princess Sophia felt that Leopold would not do, if only because he did not have any money.

Charlotte could not help feeling that her family was making plans for her behind her back again. Certainly everyone was being much warmer and more attentive to her now, and for the time being Charlotte was determined to be docile in return. As she told Mercer in her last letter before leaving for her holiday, 'I think of nothing but how I can get out of their clutches & torment them afterwards.'

CHAPTER FIFTEEN

'Princess Charlotte Is Made of Ginger-bread'

———

CHARLOTTE, HER LADIES and her servants set out from Windsor for the town of Weymouth in a column of coaches on Friday, 9 September.

If she had forgotten the warmth of the crowd's reception on the day when her father opened Parliament, she was soon reminded. She was still the most popular member of the royal family. 'Wherever I changed horses', she told Mercer, 'there were people assembled to see me, & they all looked good humoured and took off their hats'. She stopped in Andover for an early dinner and then drove on to spend the night at the Antelope Inn in Salisbury, where, she was delighted to report, the 'Bish-UP', as usual, was not in residence. She had to press through the crowd to get from her carriage to the inn, and in answer to their calls, she stood at her bedroom window for a long time with a candle held up so that they could see her.

Next day the party drove on through crowded towns and villages towards Weymouth. They stopped for dinner at Puddletown, where General Garth, who had gone ahead of them, had rented a house for himself. There was a young boy running around in the house, and the General, who said he was his adopted nephew Tom, told Charlotte after dinner that the boy would be 'much mortified' if she did not take notice of him. 'A heart of steel could not have refused that', wrote Charlotte, 'for a <u>more lovely</u> boy was never beheld'.

Skinny old Lady Rosslyn and her nieces, whom Charlotte was now calling 'Famine and the Consequences', were no longer in the room by then, but Lady Ilchester and Mrs Campbell were still there, and they were both shocked that the General had introduced the boy to the Princess.

If not also shocked, Charlotte was at least taken aback when she was told his true identity. Tom's mother was her favourite aunt, Princess Sophia, and General Garth was his father.

In the course of the next week all the ladies were surprised by the extent to which the strict old General spoiled the boy. He even allowed him to stay on for a few days after the new term had started at Harrow. But now that Charlotte knew who he was – and the General clearly knew that she knew – it was embarrassing for her to have him around. Everyone in Weymouth seemed to know who he was as well. People even gathered to have a look at him when he was taken into town to have his hair cut. As she told Mercer, Charlotte suspected that the General was making her feel uncomfortable on purpose, probably because it was an indirect way of getting his own back on her aunt for having spurned both him and their son. It was not Tom's fault, but Charlotte was relieved when he did at last go back to school.

When Charlotte reached Weymouth, the whole town was filled with people, and the military band that greeted her went on playing for an hour after she went into Gloucester Lodge. But the holiday began with what she saw as a bad omen.

The evening of her arrival, Charlotte was playing backgammon with the General when she noticed that the heart-shaped turquoise had fallen out of the ring that had been given to her by Prince August. She knew that it had still been there when she arrived at Gloucester Lodge, but she could not find it anywhere; and she never did, although the empty ring stayed on her finger throughout her stay in Weymouth. 'You don't know for such an <u>apparent</u> trifle <u>what an effect</u> it has had on me', she told Mercer, 'nor indeed how bitterly I have cried'. Charlotte was sure that the loss was a portent of ill fortune for her relationship with the Prussian Prince.

She had not had a letter from August since he left England, and she could not read the old ones because she had burned them. The only news of him came from Mercer, and most of that consisted of rumours that were soon contradicted. It was not true that he had secretly married a Miss Rumbold. Nor was it true that he had been appointed Governor of Saxony, which was also good news because, if he had been, he would never have been able to live in England.

Throughout the holiday Charlotte could only fantasise. She imagined August coming over and making a proposal to her father; and then she made herself anxious because she knew her father would refuse him. He would have to come over while Parliament was sitting. An appeal to Parliament would lead to a debate; a debate would be reported in the papers, and when the people read them they would be bound to support her against her father. If only August would make up his mind.

In one of her long outpourings to Mercer, however, Charlotte admitted that she was so miserable she might marry almost anyone. She would rather it was August. But if August did disappoint her, 'The P. of S-C <u>decidedly would be accepted by me in preference to any other Prince I have seen</u>.'

When she read in the newspapers that there had been a quarrel between two young princes at the Vienna Congress, she fantasised again and imagined it was August and Leopold quarrelling over her.

After all, she insisted unconvincingly, they were 'visibly' jealous of each other when they were in London.

To add to her worries, there was bad news about Charles Hesse, now a Captain. Although Mercer had enlisted her father's assistance, they had still failed to persuade him to send back any of Charlotte's letters or presents, and they had no hope of succeeding soon. The little hussar was not in England. According to the most reliable report, he had gone out to join Charlotte's mother and her reputedly dissolute touring party.

Yet Charlotte was determined to enjoy her holiday and put on a brave face for all the 'good people' who came to look at her. For much of the time her mood was not far from the slightly hysterical merriment with which she greeted the law officers of the Crown during the melodrama at her mother's house.

She went to performances at the Theatre Royal and the occasional ball at the Assembly Rooms; she was allowed to give dinner parties, to which she invited some of the aristocracy and gentry who came to stay in rented houses or at Ressell's Royal Hotel. Like the General, one of the constant guests at these dinners was 'the Great UP', who took a house for his family on the seafront.

On one Sunday Charlotte went to church and heard the 'Bish-UP' preach a sermon for the first time. 'I never heard so weak a voice & so bad a delivery', she wrote to Mercer. 'It is enough to spoil the very best sermon that ever was composed.' But this was nothing compared with the sermon preached on another Sunday by the apparently famous Dr Dupré. This preacher went on for forty-five minutes without notes with so many 'blunders' and 'repetitions' that he 'kept the whole pew in a <u>titter</u>'. Fortunately Charlotte was able to turn her head and hide her giggles inside one of the large bonnets made fashionable by the Grand Duchess Catherine.

There were expeditions to places of interest, such as Lulworth Castle and the monastery nearby. The monastery had been taken over by some Trappist monks who had been expelled from France during the Revolution. Charlotte rang the bell and asked to be shown round, but the porter, who was the only monk who was allowed to speak, explained that women were not allowed into the monastery. Charlotte insisted. The porter went away and spoke to the Abbot. The Abbot remembered that their rule, which excluded women, allowed the admission of royalty.

So while all the other ladies waited outside, the brightly dressed Princess was taken in among the black and white habits, shown round the monastery and its gardens and given a humble meal of milk, brown bread, vegetables and rice, which was served in wooden cups and bowls.

When she was not sailing, Charlotte's lunch was usually whatever was available at an inn, or a picnic on a beach. At one of these picnics, on the pebbled beach between Portland and Bridport, some children climbed up from the water's edge to the high bank above the beach, so that they could get a good look at the Princess. With each step they dislodged showers of pebbles which tumbled down towards the royal party.

Charlotte called up to them. 'Hallo, there! Princess Charlotte is made of ginger-bread. If you do that you'll break her.'

But Charlotte's favourite picnics were those that were served on deck when she was sailing, at which, according to one guest, she consumed large quantities of 'roast beef...with plenty of mustard!'

In her love of the sea, Charlotte was much more like her uncle the Duke of Clarence than her father, who was always seasick. She adored sailing, and she had been allowed the use of the royal yacht, which, by happy coincidence, was named, as she was, after the Queen, the *Royal Charlotte*.

One slightly rough afternoon when Charlotte and her party were out sailing, a third rate ship of the line, HMS *Leviathan*, which was anchored off Portland, sighted the royal yacht and fired a salute to her. The yacht hove to and signalled to the warship to send a boat. A boat was lowered and the captain himself came over in it to pay his respects to the Princess. When Charlotte asked to inspect his ship, he was honoured to agree.

Charlotte, two ladies and the trembling 'Bish-UP' climbed down to the boat and were rowed across through choppy water to the war-ship. By the time they reached her, to Charlotte's great amusement, they were all drenched.

As they went alongside, a chair was lowered on ropes from the great height of the main deck. But Charlotte refused to use it. She wanted to climb the steps on the ship's side like a seaman, and when she had done just that, she stood and watched while the Bishop and the ladies were hauled up one at a time in the chair.

By mid-October, when bad weather had brought an end to sail-ing, the doctors were able to report that Charlotte's health and spirits were much improved. Her knee was much better as well, as the climb up the side of *Leviathan* had demonstrated, and she had started to ride again. But it was not time to go home. The Regent was happy to have his daughter out of the way in Weymouth, and he kept her there for another two months.

There was less to do during those two months. With the hotel and the rented houses almost empty, there were fewer guests for dinner parties. On most of the long evenings the ladies sat around while Charlotte read aloud to them. The gloom that had never really gone seeped up to the surface again.

By the middle of November both Mercer and Cornelia Knight had written to Prince August, but the weeks went by without either of them receiving a reply. Charlotte could not believe that a man who had written to her so passionately did not mean at least some of what he said. She still clung to the hope that he would one day come back for her. But Mercer was clearly trying to persuade her to face up to harsh reality, and as one desperate letter succeeded another, Charlotte began to give more serious consideration to what she described as 'the next best thing...a good tempered man with good sence, with whom I could have a reasonable hope of being <u>less</u>

unhappy & comfortless than I have been in a single state.' And 'that man', she told Mercer, was 'the P of S-C.'

Yet though the Prince of Saxe-Coburg was now a practical proposition, the Prince of Prussia was still the one who inspired Charlotte's romantic longings. In a letter written a month later, on 11 December, she surpassed herself. 'If grief is to be my only share, then I will cherish, nourish, feed & love it, for nothing that comes from him can be otherwise than dear, tho' it may cut me to the soul.'

Mercer's letters have not survived, but whatever she wrote in response to that must have come close to convincing Charlotte that she was making a fool of herself and that August was a philanderer.

Shortly before she left Weymouth she wrote, 'If the plain & damning proofs are brought to me, such as must, however unwillingly, convince me of the faithlessness of the most beloved of human beings, the struggle, the effort, however painful, must be made.'

On 18 December, after a 'sad, uncomfortable' journey, on which she was driven to distraction by Lady Rosslyn's 'eternal fidgets & frights', Charlotte returned to Windsor, in time to spend Christmas with her family.

Chapter Sixteen

A Crisis at Christmas

On 21 December Charlotte received a surprise visit from her father at Cranbourne Lodge. It was a surprise in more ways than one. He listened attentively to all she had to tell him about what she had been doing in Weymouth, and he told her all the news and gossip that he thought might interest her about the family and friends. Charlotte was amazed. He could not, she said, have been 'kinder or more affectionate... It has been the most comfortable visit to me and my feelings that I have ever had...'

Two days later she received another surprise visit, this time from her old friend and tutor, and Mercer's uncle, Dr Short. The dandy doctor of divinity had been sent by her father to warn her that her mother was again making claims about the paternity of William Austin, 'the boy who she took abroad with her'.

When Dr Short had gone, Charlotte wrote to her father, thanking him for breaking the news so sensitively and asking him what she ought to do.

His answer, such as it was, came on Christmas Day, when most of the royal family was gathered at Windsor Castle. Soon after his arrival the Regent led his daughter into Princess Mary's apartment and asked Princess Mary to follow them.

As soon as the Prince had shut the door, he began by reassuring Charlotte. There was nothing to worry about while he was alive. After his death, however, her mother might claim that 'Willikin' was the true heir to the throne.

Charlotte could not dismiss the idea. Her mother, she told them, had always preferred the boy to her. She had slept with him in her bed for the first few years of his life, and even after that he had always slept on a small bed in her bedroom.

The Prince took in what his daughter said and then seemed to change the subject. He asked if Charlotte had had any particular relationship with anyone when the 18th Hussars were stationed in Windsor.

Charlotte did not stop to think. Without caution, without even asking a few questions to find out how much her father knew already. She started to tell him about Charles Hesse, and as he listened sympathetically, she opened up and told him the whole story – or almost the whole story. She admitted that Hesse had ridden beside her carriage, that they had exchanged letters and presents, that she had seen him in her mother's apartments in Kensington Palace, and even that she and Hesse had been locked in her mother's bedroom and told to enjoy themselves.

But then, as though caution had at last caught up with her, she added, 'God knows what would have become of me if he had not behaved with so much respect to me.'

Her father spoke in sorrow without a hint of anger. 'My dear child, it is Providence alone that has saved you.'

It looked as though he believed her, even though he knew that the rest of the world would not. But she cannot have been telling the whole truth. By her own admission to Mercer, she still cared about her hussar because she had been 'so intimate' with him. Besides, judging by his subsequent record with other ladies, including royalty,

Charles Hesse was not the sort of man to be respectful when locked up alone with a lady in a bedroom.

For no apparent reason, the Prince asked if the Duke of Brunswick knew about Captain Hesse.

Charlotte said no, and then added that the Duke had warned her about her mother and had said he was sure that 'Willikin' was her child.

As if by way of finding out who the father might be, the Prince then asked how much Charlotte knew about her mother's lovers; the answer, surprisingly, was quite a lot. She was able to name most of the men mentioned in 'the delicate investigation', although the only one she felt sure about was Captain Manby.

After that the Prince brought the conversation to an end. But there was still nothing but sadness and sympathy in his voice. Charlotte, he said, had done wrong in her relationship with Hesse. She had let him down, she had let herself down and, what was worse, she had let her country down. But he had not come to reproach her. His job now was to save her.

The Prince went back to London. His bewildered daughter ate Christmas dinner with the rest of the family, and then Princess Mary led her back into her apartment to continue the kindly interrogation.

Princess Mary asked if Charlotte's mother was in favour of her marriage to the Hereditary Prince of Orange. Charlotte said that she had not been to start with, because she hated the House of Orange, but that by the time the engagement was broken off she had learned to accept it.

The topic turned to Hesse again. Did Charlotte really not realise what her mother was up to when she organised their romance? By the implications in her questions, Princess Mary made it clear that in this at least she agreed with her brother. The Princess of Wales was making sure that, if she ever needed it, she would have enough evidence to discredit her daughter.

Charlotte went back to Cranbourne Lodge haunted by what she described as 'a presentiment of evil'. Next day, Princess Mary, who was compiling a memorandum of all these conversations, called on her accompanied by the Queen.

This time all they wanted to know was who Charlotte thought was the father of 'Willikin'. Charlotte's best guess was Captain Manby, but she also said that there was just a chance that it was her father. She was too young at the time to remember for sure, but she thought there were two or three nights when her mother stayed at Carlton House after she had moved to Blackheath. The Queen and her daughter left Cranbourne Lodge even more dismayed than they had meant to make Charlotte.

Clearly Charlotte did not know about the Mrs Austin who came over regularly to Blackheath to visit 'Willikin', and she seems to have forgotten the findings of the two 'investigations'. The Princess of Wales had never said that she was the mother of 'Willikin', or that her husband was his father. It was the Douglases who had said that she said it, and the Douglases had been proved to be perjurers. If Charlotte had only remembered that, she might just have wondered whether her father's story was true or not.

⁂

Charlotte's father had succeeded in frightening her. Yet at the same time she was confused by his uncharacteristic sympathy and kindness. Mercer and Earl Grey both said that they thought he was trying to make her feel insecure, so that she would be easier to manipulate when he renewed his attempts to make her marry the Hereditary Prince of Orange.

For the next few weeks, however, the Prince Regent did nothing to follow up his success. At the beginning of January he went to Brighton. Throughout the month the only time Charlotte heard from him was on her nineteenth birthday, when he sent her a note explaining that an attack of gout prevented him from attending her little party.

But Mercer and Earl Grey had worried her with their suspicions. On 17 January, when she was dining at Frogmore, she asked her uncle Frederick, the Duke of York, if he thought her father still wanted to marry her to the young Prince of Orange.

The Duke did not know, but he felt that, even if he did, she had nothing to worry about. None of the other members of her family would allow her to marry against her will. Besides, he explained, there was an important congress being held in Vienna. Many new alliances were being made. Wellington and Castlereagh could easily come back with better offers from other princes.

Charlotte thanked him politely. She knew much more about the Congress of Vienna than he realised. She had just received a letter from her other uncle Frederick, the Duke of Brunswick. In it, as in any letter to a niece, 'the Black Duke' reported his family news and told her that he had seen the Grand Duchess Catherine, who spoke warmly of her and sent her best wishes. But he also gave a detailed report on the progress at the Congress of Vienna. He outlined the conflicting interests, described the various proposals under discussion and listed the possible consequences of each; and he gave his own opinion on the agreements that he thought would be best for Britain. For a Princess whose own family was still treating her as a child, it was good to be reminded that the ruling families in the rest of Europe regarded her as an intelligent adult and respected her as a future queen.

On the day after her dinner at Frogmore, Charlotte received another, much less welcome, letter from Europe. It came in a package delivered secretly through Cornelia Knight. It was a letter from Prince August of Prussia, and it was accompanied by the miniature portrait and the ring that she had given to him.

Military duty, he told her, prevented him from confessing the deep feelings that she had inspired in him, and he was sending back her charming portrait because keeping it would only serve to make his sense of regret even worse.

It was as kind a way of saying goodbye as he could manage, and it may have been true. Perhaps his duty did come first. Perhaps Charlotte really had aroused feelings that the Prince had not known since his parting from Madame Récamier. If she did, he never knew them again. When he died, aged sixty-three, Prince August was still unmarried.

Charlotte wrote to Mercer. 'If anything was further wanted to <u>decide</u> the affair, this does it.'

She was surprised by how calmly Miss Knight was taking it, given that it brought 'termination' to one of her 'favourite schemes'. Indeed, like Miss Knight, who returned the compliment, Charlotte was surprised and pleased by how well she was taking it herself. 'I know I feel satisfied with myself, & that is one step, & a great one, to getting comfortable if not happy again.'

Two days later it was clear that Charlotte had already set her mind, if not her heart, on marrying Prince Leopold. At another dinner with the Duchess of York, she decided to find out if the Duchess really was as much in favour of Leopold as her aunt Sophia said she was.

Charlotte opened the conversation by asking the Duchess of York her opinion of the Prince of Orange. The Duchess did not like him; neither did she approve of the manner in which the Prince Regent had been forcing him on Charlotte. In her opinion, her father ought to invite several princes to London and let Charlotte make a choice.

Charlotte then mentioned Prince Leopold.

The Duchess 'colored beyond anything', and said, 'I beg as a favour you will never let it be known you mentioned him to me, for as I happen to be nearly related to him, particularly intimate with him, like him very much, and am in constant correspondence with him, it would be directly said that I managed this match.'

Charlotte knew that she had at least two allies in the royal family. A week earlier, when it had not mattered so much, Princess Mary had abandoned her enigmatic attitude and 'launched forth vehemently' in praise of Leopold, partly because of his reputation as a man of the highest character, and partly because he came from a very old family. Then the Duke of York revealed himself as an ally, although, like Mercer, he advised Charlotte to keep quiet for the time being.

It was good advice. No proposal was likely to succeed with the Regent if it contradicted one of his own. But now that she had made up her mind, Charlotte did not feel inclined to wait. She persuaded Mercer that it would do no harm if 'the Leo', as she now called him, were to come over uninvited, and on 3 February she wrote to Mercer asking her to make it happen.

> Before you named it I was hourly going to propose to you what certainly nothing could have authorised me or prompted me to have done, but our long intimacy & your kind affection for me. It was this, whether you thought you could by <u>any means send him a hint that his presence at this moment</u> in England would be of service to <u>his views</u> if they were the same as 6 months ago.

Next day, as if in justification, she wrote:

> As I care for no man in the world now, I don't see what it signifies as to my marrying one day sooner or later except for escaping the present evils that surround me. I don't see what there is against my connecting myself with the most calm & perfect indifference to a man who, I know, has the highest & best character possible in every way, & is extremely prepossessing in his figure and appearance & who <u>certainly did like</u> me.

A few days later, however, the Prince Regent revealed his hand, proving not only that Mercer and the Duke of York were giving good advice but also that Mercer and Earl Grey had been justified in their suspicions after Christmas.

The Prince summoned Mercer and her father to Brighton, ostensibly to discuss their attempts to recover Charlotte's letters from Captain Hesse. If those letters were to fall into the wrong hands, particularly her mother's, he said, she would be ruined. He therefore appointed Lord Keith officially as his representative with instructions to interview Captain Hesse and find the letters.

After that the Prince turned abruptly to the possibility of a marriage with the Hereditary Prince of Orange. For Charlotte, he said, this was now 'the only means of saving her reputation, getting out of her mother's hands, and making herself quite happy'.

Mercer answered without a hint of respect. 'It is not actually necessary to marry one man', she said, 'to apologise for writing love letters to another'.

The Prince said nothing. Emboldened by her own impatient impudence, Mercer went on, 'The last time Princess Charlotte talked to me about it, she said that so far from repenting the step she had taken, she would rather continue to suffer all the restraint and privations she had these last six months than marry the Prince of Orange.'

The Prince did not seem to be convinced, or else he did not want to be. Mercer left the meeting frustrated. No matter what anyone thought or said, the Regent was clearly determined to have his own way.

❄

Having heard from several aunts as well as Mercer that the 'Orange match' was on again, Charlotte wrote to her father. It was a humble and respectful letter, but it was firm. Although she accepted that she could not marry 'as the rest of the world do', she was not prepared to do so without 'esteem and regard'. As a result, a marriage with the Hereditary Prince of Orange was out of the question.

Her father wrote back. Charlotte, he said, was only refusing the Prince of Orange because she had been exposed to 'the council and advice of mischievous, false and wicked persons'. She could not afford to say no. Once her letters to Captain Hesse were exposed, she would not be in a position to marry anyone.

Charlotte sent a copy of this letter to Mercer. On 26 February, after she had received Mercer's answer, she wrote again, 'I remain firm & unshaken, & no arguments, no threats shall ever bend me to marry this detested Duchman. You are quite right in your letter of today that my letter had not convinced. I begin almost to despair of what will.'

On the same day, up at the castle, Charlotte read her father's letter to the Queen. The Queen, unusually for her, burst into tears. The Queen wrote to her eldest son. Several of his brothers and sisters wrote to him as well. The Prince Regent was at bay in Brighton.

And then came the news that brought all negotiations in Brighton, Windsor, London, Vienna and anywhere else in Europe to a standstill. On 1 March Napoleon had escaped from the island of Elba. He had landed in France. His old army was rallying round him.

The Congress of Vienna broke up. The nations of Northern Europe made ready to go back to war.

Amid the anxiety on every other front, the emergency brought one relief to Charlotte. Captain Hesse came home to rejoin his regiment. Mercer and her father found and confronted him. He convinced them that all letters had been burned. The trunk that contained them was empty. With but two exceptions, every present that he had ever received from Charlotte was returned to Mercer. One exception was a turquoise ring, which he first said was still in his baggage and then said had been lost when he was wearing it round his plume in battle. The other was the watch. But Charlotte did not think that either of these was significant enough to be incriminating. The matter was at an end. The little hussar was no longer a threat.

On 14 May Mercer received a letter from Leopold. It was the answer to the one she had sent him much earlier, but it had taken a long time to reach her. It had been written in Vienna on 28 April. Leopold had little hope of going back to England now. He was about to rejoin the Russian army and take up his old command. But if Mercer could assure him that he would be welcome to the Princess, he would do all that he could to come.

Mercer wrote back. She did not dare to give him that assurance. Making suggestions was as much as she could risk. If she was caught negotiating a royal marriage, she would never be allowed to see Charlotte again.

But on 2 June, before her letter reached him, Leopold wrote another to Mercer. After thinking about it, he had decided not to risk coming to England uninvited. If he did, he might offend the Regent, and without the Regent's goodwill, his dream could never be fulfilled.

But by then Leopold would not have been able to come to England anyway. Napoleon had assembled 125,000 men in northern France. Further north, along the border, the allies were waiting. In another two weeks they would be fully prepared for a combined invasion. Meanwhile, if Napoleon struck first, they were almost ready to receive him. The Austrians were to the east of Strasbourg, in a long line between Basle and Worms. The Russians were in the centre, north-west of Frankfort. The Prussians were south-west of them, below Namur and Liege. The British, Dutch, Hanoverians and Brunswickers were to the west between Brussels and the sea.

And most of the men who had played leading parts in Charlotte's short life were with them. Leopold was with the Russians in the centre; August was with Blücher's Prussians; Charles Hesse, George FitzClarence, the Prince of Orange and the Duke of Brunswick were with Wellington beyond Brussels.

No matter what route Napoleon chose, at least one of them would be in harm's way.

CHAPTER SEVENTEEN

Waterloo

———⟶———

LATE IN THE afternoon of 20 June 1815 a rumour began to spread through the great London mansions of Mayfair and St James's. Nathan Rothschild, the banker, had received a report through his many agents on the continent and had sent a messenger to the Prime Minister.

Some said he had then gone down to the Stock Exchange with an expression of deep melancholy on his face. Since everyone was sure that he would be the first to know if anything had happened to the army, the brokers feared the worst and started to sell. When prices fell, Rothschild stepped in and bought. But that, if it was true, was the only indication that the news was good.

Charlotte was by then living at Warwick House again – although not even with the same limited freedom that she had known before. The entrance had been blocked. The only way in or out of Warwick House now was through Carlton House and the courtyard that divided them.

When the rumour reached her, Charlotte asked for a message to be sent to the Colonial Office. It was addressed to Lord Bathurst, the Secretary of State for War and the Colonies, and it asked him to send on any news to her as soon as it reached him, even if it came in the middle of the night – 'the Princess being exceedingly anxious to receive tidings and particularly to know the fate of some of her friends.'

But throughout the night and for most of the next day there was no official news. All that anyone could add to the rumour was that Nathan Rothschild had apparently received a copy of a Dutch newspaper containing a vague report of an allied victory.

In the evening the Prince Regent went round from Carlton House to attend a ball at 16 St James's Square. His hostess was Mrs Edmund Boehm, whose husband had made a vast fortune in the sugar trade, and the ball was the pinnacle of her ambitious social career. At last, her guests included not only the Regent but also his brother the Duke of York and her neighbour Lord Castlereagh.

The Regent led off the dancing. Before the first dance was over, however, a commotion in the square brought the music to a standstill and the dancers to the windows. There were cheering people running out of the side streets. An open carriage was clattering towards the house. By the light of the tapers that running footmen were carrying ahead of it, the dancers could see that it contained a young soldier dressed in the simple scarlet coatee of a staff officer. He was Major the Hon. Henry Percy, aide-de-camp to the Duke of Wellington. Percy leapt out of the carriage and ran into the house and up the stairs, carrying what looked like a short but broad roll of cloth under each arm.

He crossed the drawing room and knelt in front of the Regent panting. 'Victory... Victory, Sire!'

As he spoke, he dropped two captured eagles – French regimental colours with golden eagles on the tips of their poles.

Then he took out a small purple velvet bag that had been given to him a week earlier by a young lady at the Duchess of Richmond's ball in Brussels. From this he drew out the Duke of Wellington's despatch.

The Regent took the despatch and retired into another room with the Foreign Secretary. When he returned he was in tears, and for once his tears were justified.

Mrs Boehm's muttering guests fell silent. Castlereagh read the despatch aloud. Four days ago, the allies had destroyed Napoleon's army at Waterloo. But the cost had been terrible. There had not yet been time to make out a complete list of the officers who had been killed or wounded, but those listed in the despatch, together with those that Henry Percy could remember, were still so many that there was no one in the room who had not lost a kinsman or a friend.

The Prince Regent returned at once to Carlton House, accompanied by the Foreign Secretary. All the guests went home after them, hurrying to bring the grim but glorious news to their families. Mr and Mrs Boehm were left alone with the musicians, extra servants and a huge uneaten supper.

At Warwick House, the news was, for the most part, a relief. Napoleon had decided to strike at the right flank and try to take on the allies one at a time. So the Russians were too far away to be engaged – Leopold was safe. Wellington and Blücher were the only commanders who had been able to combine, and theirs were the armies that had suffered the casualties. Among these, Charlotte learned, both Charles Hesse and the Hereditary Prince of Orange had been wounded, although neither so severely that his life was in danger. But there was also a loss, and it was a loss that brought back the gloom that Warwick House had not seen since the death of Mrs Gagarin.

Two days before the battle of Waterloo, in an attempt to halt the French advance, the Duke of Brunswick had been killed leading his black cavalry in a charge at Quatre Bras. The little duchy had lost another duke to Napoleon.

The Prince Regent had forbidden Charlotte to communicate with her mother, but, in the circumstances, he allowed one letter.

Charlotte never received a reply. Several weeks later, however, she received a letter of condolence from Lady Charlotte Campbell, who was still a member of her mother's entourage. Lady Charlotte kept the answer.

> ... It was a grievous circumstance – a dreadful, irremediable loss to me, for the great possess few real friends. In him I had a warm and constant one, allied, too, by the closest ties of blood. I loved him with the fondest affection, & am confident he returned the sentiment. His death was so glorious, so completely what he always desired for himself – that if it was decreed that he should so early in life quit this world, he could not close his career more gloriously or more worthy of a hero as he was & of that father & that blood he descended from... I trust my mother continues well, & that she has not been very much shocked by the death of her brother. I hope she has got a letter. <u>I was permitted</u> to write to her on the sad event.

Grief did not, however, distract Charlotte from what was now her only important objective. By the time she wrote that letter, she had written to the Prime Minister asking him to represent her formally with her father and request him to offer her hand in marriage to Prince Leopold of Saxe-Coburg. If he did not agree, she warned, she would remain a spinster and refuse all other suitors.

This time the Prince Regent's excuse was 'the state of the Continent and the negotiations' that followed the exile of Napoleon to St Helena. This, he said, was not the moment to consider such a proposal. In his report to Charlotte, Lord Liverpool told her that for the time being he felt there was no more he could do; the matter would have to be 'postponed for his Royal Highness's further consideration'.

When the Duke of York heard what had happened he agreed with the Prime Minister and advised Charlotte to be patient. He was in touch with Leopold and knew that he was about to join the allied army in Paris. Duty might well prevent him from coming to England for a few months anyway, and meanwhile Charlotte was about to be sent away for another seaside exile in Weymouth. The Duke's advice was to wait until November, when Parliament would be sitting again, and then 'make another push'.

Chapter Eighteen

Waiting in Weymouth

A T FIRST CHARLOTTE found it easy enough to follow the advice to be patient with her father. But it was not so easy to be patient with Leopold. As soon as she reached Weymouth, she wrote to Mercer telling her that 'the Leo' was in Paris, and begging her to write to him, although she added, 'Preach up prudence. A false step now I feel would ruin all.'

In the weeks and then months that followed, Mercer wrote encouraging letters to Leopold, Leopold wrote back to Mercer, Mercer passed on what he had said to Charlotte, and in her answers Charlotte became more and more eager and less and less inclined to go on waiting.

On 21 August, late at night, she wrote:

Your accounts of him constantly at Lady Castlereagh's stupid suppers does not astonish me... Oh why should he not come over, it is so near & it is but a run over of a few hours. I quite languish for his arrival. He is really wrong in keeping back as he does. Having got your letter what more can he wish for to bring him? Don't you know an old proverb wh. says, 'Hope long delayed maketh the heart sick'. What does he mean about a <u>crisis</u>? I see & hear of nothing that is like it.

Just over a week later, after Mercer had induced Leopold to share his feelings with her, Charlotte wrote, 'I will tell you candidly that I am <u>delighted</u>, not to say <u>charmed & flattered</u> at what Leo writes about his sentiments and feelings for me, & the way in wh. he expresses himself is peculiarly pleasing.'

After another month she was beginning to hope that Leopold had decided to come over, and yet at the same time both she and Mercer were worried that someone was advising him against it – it was possible that 'hints might have reached him through the Prussians' about Prince August, or that somebody had told him about Charles Hesse. If he did come, Charlotte wanted Mercer to meet him and explain.

> If you see him long enough to have such confidential & various conversation with him, I allow you...to <u>clear all that up to him</u> in the best manner you please, & even if you think it necessary, to hint also at Hesse's affair since I was <u>quite clear</u> (that unless he is well prepared & armed against all the lies & different things that will be told him) he will not know what to believe, who to credit, or how to act.

A week later, still hoping that Leopold was coming soon, Charlotte was in a mood to be devious. She told Mercer, 'I give you <u>carte blanche</u> if you see him, to say & do all that circumstances will allow & require. Don't send me any of his letters, let me see them when we meet, that you may <u>honorably</u> be able to keep to saying you <u>never forwarded any letters to me</u>.'

Yet amid all the frustration and disappointment, the news that raised Charlotte's hopes the highest was not about Leopold but about

'Slender Billy'. It was announced in Holland that the Hereditary Prince of Orange was engaged to marry the Tsar's younger sister, the Grand Duchess Anne.

The Dutch fleet was to be united with the Russian fleet. For those who were inclined to suspect a conspiracy, and who did not know how much Charlotte detested the young Prince of Orange, it looked as though the scheming Grand Duchess Catherine had brought about the breach between them as part of a long-term Russian plan. But for Charlotte the news was nothing more than a merciful release. Her father no longer had a pet plan to promote above any other.

But then she heard that several other eligible princes had been seen in London and at Windsor. On 14 October she wrote, 'I have such a dread of all foreign Princes, the sight as well as the name of them alarm me from the idea of some intrigue or other going on for my marrying someone of them.'

By then it was a while since Mercer had heard from Leopold, and a week later Charlotte began to despair. 'His silence to you is now what <u>surprises & occupies</u> me the <u>most</u> for you <u>ought</u> to have heard long before this.'

November came. It was the month when Parliament was sitting again, the month in which the Duke of York advised Charlotte to make 'another push'. But Mercer heard nothing from Leopold, and while Charlotte waited in Weymouth she underwent what she described as an alarming adventure.

On Friday, 10 November, between four and five o'clock in the evening, the Princess was looking out of her dressing room window when she saw a young gentleman with his right arm in a leather sling walking on the esplanade. He looked exactly like Charles Hesse. Charlotte took out her telescope and had another look at him as he walked back. It *was* Charles Hesse.

As Charlotte told Mercer, 'What to do was the next question.' Was he there because he knew Charlotte was there? What would happen if the Prince Regent found out he had been there, even if he and Charlotte never met?

Charlotte went to General Garth and told him all that he needed to know. The old General went out, found the young Captain and sat down with him on a bench. Garth asked why Hesse was in Weymouth. The answer was that, while still recovering from his wound, Hesse was on his way to stay with friends in Cornwall. He had stopped off for the night in Weymouth because he had never seen it before. Garth then asked him if he knew that Princess Charlotte was staying in Weymouth. Hesse said that he did not. Garth believed him. In that case, said the General, it was the Captain's duty to leave town at once. Hesse agreed. He was due to leave next day at noon, but if that was not enough he would try to find a way of leaving earlier. Garth said that it was enough.

Next day Charlotte watched as Charles Hesse walked past Gloucester Lodge to join the Exeter coach. That evening, to guard against any future accusation of subterfuge, she wrote to the Duke of York and told him what had happened.

Soon afterwards, Hesse left England and rejoined the entourage of Charlotte's mother. After her death, he lived in Italy, where he had several eminent lovers, including the Queen of Naples, whose husband eventually had him escorted out of the kingdom by carabinieri. He also fought a number of duels, in the last of which he was killed by another bastard, Count Leon, whose father was Napoleon.

The Duke of York wrote back to Charlotte. 'I can easily conceive how unexpected and unpleasant Mr H.'s appearance at Weymouth must have been to you, and think that in the very awkward situation in which it placed you, you acted quite right in sacrificing your own feelings, however disagreeable it must have been to you in confessing to General Garth the delicacy of your situation.'

Charlotte was pleased by her uncle's approval, but while Leopold's silence continued, the Duke's next letter brought even greater comfort. 'You may be assured, dearest Charlotte, that tho' absent you are not forgot, and that your real friends are doing everything in their power to serve you and further your wishes, and I cannot but be confident that the patience and acquiescence which you have shown in all the arrangements which have been made for you, will have a proper effect.'

'I think, that he does know something he don't like to say', wrote Charlotte hopefully to Mercer. But as December came and went there was still no sign of it, and Charlotte's continuing anxiety can only have been made more poignant by the news that Mercer was in love.

The man who had won Mercer's heart, and who had lost his own heart to her, was Auguste Charles Joseph, Count de Flahault de la Billarderie. He had served in the French army in both Spain and Russia, where he had been appointed an aide-de-camp to Napoleon, and he had rejoined the Emperor when he returned from Elba and served with him again at Waterloo. Like many of Napoleon's closest supporters, he had left France as soon as the allies restored the Bourbon King Louis-Philippe to the throne. Since he had been educated in Scotland and spoke English fluently, he had gone to live in Edinburgh; it was there that he met his beautiful Scots heiress.

The thirty-year-old Count de Flahault was everything that Mercer was looking for: handsome, worldly, cultured and charming. It was widely believed that his father was Prince Talleyrand, who was having an affair with his mother before he was born; and in qualities and abilities he was certainly much closer to the great statesman than the provincial count whose title he inherited. He was so confident and clever that, despite his recent setback, he was clearly destined for further success. And as if these gifts were not enough, Mercer's father added to his dangerous attraction by disapproving of him because he was a Bonapartist. So while Mercer was being courted by her Count, Charlotte went on languishing in Weymouth. She spent Christmas Day there without a single member of her family for company, and it was not until New Year's Day that she and her ladies climbed into their carriages to ride back to Windsor and Cranbourne Lodge.

On 6 January Charlotte drove down to Brighton with the Queen and two of her aunts. The next day was her twentieth birthday, and the Prince Regent was giving a party for her at his pavilion. In the course of the evening she made 'another push' on behalf of Prince Leopold, and this time her father made no objection.

Knowing that the Regent could remember things as he wanted them to be rather than as they were, Charlotte wrote to him as soon as she returned to Cranbourne Lodge, repeating on paper exactly what had been said in Brighton. Her excuse was that her shyness often prevented her from expressing herself clearly, and 'in the present instance' she therefore felt that it was essential 'to have recourse to writing'. After reminding her father that he had once told her he would leave the choice to her, she went on. 'Thus encouraged I no longer hesitate in declaring my partiality for the Prince of Coburg – assuring you that no one will be more steady or consistent in their present & last engagement than myself.'

But there was no need to worry. The Duke of York had indeed known something. At the end of the previous year the Regent had been making enquiries. He consulted Lord Castlereagh, who had been impressed by Leopold at the Vienna Congress, and Lord Lauderdale, who had got to know him better than anyone else when he was last in England. Both agreed that he was a man of the highest principles and an ideal husband for their future queen, and further-more Lauderdale could confirm that he was 'partial to the young lady'.

The answer to Charlotte's letter was the news that her father had written to Leopold summoning him to England, and that his letter was accompanied by a letter from Castlereagh explaining to Leopold that the Regent intended to offer him his daughter's hand in marriage.

All that was needed now was for the courier to find Leopold. He was no longer in Paris, but he had not, as some said, gone to Russia. When the courier reached Coburg he was told that Leopold had gone to Berlin, and it was there that he found him, in the middle of February.

By then Charlotte was exasperated with waiting. On 21 February she wrote to Mercer. 'By accurate calculation & <u>measurement</u> of the <u>distance</u> between Berlin & Coburg I find <u>no reason</u> (except the bad roads) for his not being here now.'

Charlotte's calculation was correct. The day on which she wrote that letter was also the day on which Leopold landed at Dover and drove to London. This time there was no need to take rooms above a grocer's shop in Marylebone High Street. This time the Prince Regent was paying. Leopold checked in at the Clarendon Hotel in Bond Street, where a suite had been reserved for him.

CHAPTER NINETEEN

'An Inappropriate Relationship'

———◇———

L EOPOLD WAS IN England for five days before Charlotte saw him. He spent his first day in bed at his London hotel suffering from what Charlotte described as 'rheumatism in his head', and he was still suffering when he left next day to stay with the Prince Regent at his pavilion in Brighton. But, as Charlotte told Mercer, 'He says he waits to <u>see me</u> to cure <u>that</u> and all other ailments.'

At last, on 26 February, Charlotte drove down to Brighton, accompanied, as was becoming usual, by her grandmother and a couple of aunts. In the evening they dined with Leopold and the Prince Regent. Everyone was 'in high spirits', and everyone was impressed by Leopold's charm and dignity as well as his good looks. As Lady Ilchester put it, 'imagination cannot picture a countenance more justifiable of love at first sight'.

The Queen was so taken with the Prince that she declined her usual game of cards after dinner and chose to sit talking instead – although she had little chance to talk to Leopold. Charlotte and he were totally absorbed in each other, anxiously reassuring, eagerly planning, and talking all the time in French, since Leopold's French was much better than his English, and Charlotte's was better than her German.

Late that night, when the party was over, Charlotte sat down in her room at the Royal Pavilion and wrote to Mercer.

> I find him quite charming, & I go to bed happier than I have ever done yet in my life... I am certainly a most fortunate creature & have to bless God. A Pss. never, I believe, set out in life (or married) with such prospects of happiness, real domestic ones like other people. I'm so very grateful at my lot I cannot express it sufficiently to you. All he said was so very charming & so right & so everything in short I could wish. I will report you further progress, but I don't know if I shall have much time to write again till I get back to Cranburn.

After all that happiness and harmony, however, the letter ended on an inadvertently discordant note. 'I must not forget to tell you', wrote Charlotte, 'that I am <u>desired by him</u> to <u>scold you</u> for your <u>intimacy</u> with Flahaud. He knows him personally & disapproves highly of him, & thinks his acquaintance is likely to do you no good, altho' he readily admits his many agrements in society.'

Mercer's letters have not survived, but there must have been resentment, reproach or even more in her answer to that, and it looks as though someone had told her that Charlotte was expressing her own disapproval as well.

On 2 March, Charlotte wrote from Cranbourne Lodge:

> You know I must love you always just as much & just the same, independently of who you may live with and what your society may be. I never have presumed & never should think with anyone, however intimate, to interfere with their society, as I do not charge my friends or make them dependent upon that. Therefore for God sake do not fancy I was or ever am in the least angry with your intimacy with Flahaud. What you were told as my having said is a

downright lie, as <u>to no</u> one did I ever express myself in that or any other way on the subject, <u>still less</u> ever thought so.

Charlotte was sure that 'much of the mischief' had been caused by her father's latest mistress, Lady Hertford, who was 'scandalised' by the extent to which Flahault was being received in society, particularly by Whigs. But she also suspected that her father had helped to start the rumour that she had been criticising Mercer. The Regent had always been wary of Mercer, and he regarded her as a defiant influence. 'You yourself, my dear love', wrote Charlotte, 'must know & have been long aware that the P.R. does and did not like you'.

Yet, despite her wish to disassociate herself from her fiancé's warnings about Flahault, Charlotte said nothing to oppose or dismiss them. 'What I wrote to you, my best M., was not from myself but from Coburg. He wished me to tell you fairly that such an intimacy did you harm in the eyes of the world, that he knew him personally both for a Jacobin & a man of bad conduct & principles in regard to women.'

The last bit was probably the true cause of 'Coburg's' disapproval. There was a lot that Charlotte never knew.

In the first place, Flahault had been an aide-de-camp to Napoleon, a post for which Leopold had once applied. Secondly, and more importantly, Flahault had been established in his military career by the influence of his beautiful and powerful mistress, Queen Hortense, who, as the daughter of the Empress Josephine and the wife of Napoleon's brother Louis, was the Emperor's step-daughter as well as his sister-in-law. It was Hortense who had fascinated and seduced the young Leopold when he first went to Paris with his brother in October 1807, and it was Flahault who replaced Leopold in her affections and her bed after his departure in March 1808. When Leopold next visited Hortense in Paris, in 1814, there was a three-year-old boy running round the house, the future Duke de Morny, whose father was Flahault. Leopold's animosity towards Flahault had more to do with envy and rivalry than disdain for his politics and morals.

No matter what anyone said, however, Mercer was much too intelligent and self-confident to be persuaded by prejudice, and Charlotte was obviously aware of her indignation. Her anxiety to retain Mercer's trust and affection is evident in every letter that she wrote to her during the next two months.

As a mark of her own trust, Charlotte continued to take Mercer into her confidence. At the end of March she wrote:

> The P.R. touched upon Hesse's business with me & begged I would tell it to C., wh. I did after much difficulty one night. He took it uncommonly well & was very kind as he saw me so much distressed... He told me he should tell the P.R. I had told him the affair, wh. he was <u>sorry</u> for, as it was past & long gone by, & should not be thought or talked of any more...

In most of the letters Charlotte was also eager to blame her father for any discord and assure her friend that Leopold meant well by her. At the end of March, when Mercer was hoping to visit her in Windsor, she wrote:

> I honestly confess to you I am <u>afraid</u> to ask you to come yet (for ever so short a time) as there is so much <u>jealousy</u> & suspicion as well as <u>misrepresentation</u> afloat. Things are not as comfortable as I could wish them to be or as they ought to be, but indeed I cannot blame Coburg, for I think I never saw a more amiable, affectionate, <u>sensible, quiet</u>, reasonable (or, in short) charming person than he is. But I see his situation will be a most awkward & distressing as well as difficult one, & he feels it himself, for the P.R. is certainly for restricting us considerably as to society & I know he has been poisoning his ears about you.

Leopold, she said, was torn between his indebtedness to Mercer and the need to be deferential to his future father-in-law. 'C. has a great horror of appearing ungrateful & insensible to you & your kindness, but yet I see the P.R. has been putting him on his <u>guard</u>...'

Yet Charlotte was sure that all the disapproval and distrust would vanish as soon as she and Leopold were married. 'When we are more together', she wrote soon afterwards, 'I really do think that he will be everything that <u>we</u> can wish, as he will <u>see</u> with his <u>own eyes</u>, <u>hear</u> with his <u>own ears</u>, & be convinced of the truth & falsehood of things, for he has a good head & a good heart, & is convinced you are attached to me...'

Charlotte was so desperate to reassure her friend that she even showed her some of Leopold's letters, although she warned, 'For God in Heaven's sake never let it be known or suspected I ever showed you any...' And the gamble seems to have succeeded. On 11 April she wrote, 'I am delighted to read your opinion and hear all you say about Leo & his letters. He rises & they do still higher in my estimation & opinion from what your impression of them is.'

There is no knowing how many letters Mercer saw, but there were certainly plenty to choose from. The Prince Regent kept Charlotte and Leopold apart as much as possible. Leopold was in Brighton and Charlotte was in Windsor, and they only met occasionally when Charlotte drove down to the pavilion for dinner. Their courtship, such as it was, was conducted mostly through letters. As their wedding day approached, they were still as eager and optimistic as they had been when they first dined together in Brighton, but, as Leopold readily admitted, they hardly knew each other any better.

Nevertheless, in the planning and preparation for their life together, there was much to keep them busy. In Brighton Leopold spent several hours each day learning English, at which his vocabulary and grammar were soon much better than his pronunciation. But he was still unwell. Meeting up with Charlotte had not, as he hoped, cured everything, and nor had the hot baths which the

Regent's doctor had told him to take every other day. Within a fortnight of his arrival in Brighton he had written to Coburg to ask his personal physician, Dr Christian Stockmar, to join him.

Perceptive, practical and good-humoured, little Dr Stockmar was a highly qualified young physician who had taken over the military hospital in Coburg on the outbreak of hostilities with France. He had then served as a regimental surgeon with the Prussian army, and since the end of the war he had formed a close friendship with Leopold. Within days of his arrival in Brighton he had superseded Leopold's equerry, Baron Hardenbroek, as his closest adviser. When Leopold and Charlotte assembled their own staff, Stockmar became the Prince's Secretary, Comptroller of his Household and Keeper of his Privy Purse; he remained his confidant until, many years later, Leopold sent him back from Brussels to London to become mentor to his niece Victoria.

CHAPTER TWENTY

'Bless Me, What a Crowd'

————

As soon as Leopold was naturalised as a British subject, the Prince Regent commissioned him a general in the British army and offered to raise him to the peerage as Duke of Kendal. Leopold refused the dukedom, but this was his only modest defiance. He acquiesced in everything when the marriage contract was drawn up, and he took no part in the financial discussions. That was left to the Regent and his government.

After much debate and indecision, Parliament agreed to provide the royal couple with two houses. Their London residence was to be Camelford House, a meagre brick building on the corner of Park Lane and Oxford Street, which had dark, little rooms, a narrow hall and only one staircase. The house had been the home of the second Lord Camelford, a cousin of William Pitt and a notorious duellist, who had died of a wound there twelve years earlier, after an encounter with Captain Best in Holland Park. Charlotte though it was much too small. 'It will do for this season', she told Mercer, 'but really for the next we must look out for another'.

By contrast, their home was to be Claremont near Esher in Surrey, which Charlotte thought was 'the most beautiful house and place possible'. She had visited it twice when she first went to stay with the Duke and Duchess of York at Oatlands, and by what looked like good luck, the most recent of its many unhappy owners, Charles Rose Ellis, had put it up for sale because his beautiful wife had just died there in childbirth.

For furniture, silver, linen, china and all the other household equipment, Parliament voted a generous single payment of £60,000, which was almost as much as it paid for Claremont. For living expenses and the cost of their household, Leopold was to be given £50,000 a year, and in addition Charlotte was to have £10,000 a year 'pin money' to cover the cost of her clothes and the payment of her ladies and her personal maids.

Charlotte was restrained in the composition of her new household. She settled for six footmen, not eight as her father suggested, and their state livery was to be simple green, not gaudy crimson and green like his. She was also loyal. She kept on many of the people who had been closest to her at Windsor and Warwick House. Among them, Mrs Campbell was to be lady-in-waiting, despite 279 applications for the job; Mercer's uncle the Rev. Dr Short was to be chaplain; and Mrs Louis, of course, was to stay on as dresser.

Mrs Louis was kept busy as the wedding day approached. Charlotte's dress, ordered by the Queen and made by Mrs Triand of Bolton Street, did not quite fit; a few subtle alterations were required. But the dress was ready in plenty of time. The ceremony was postponed more than once because of the Prince Regent's gout.

At last the date was set. It was to be 2 May. On 22 April Leopold drove up from Brighton to Windsor and settled in at Upper Lodge. But he did not meet up with Charlotte until Princess Mary's fortieth birthday party three days later at Frogmore.

On 29 April everyone set out for London. The Queen and her daughters drove up from Windsor Castle to Buckingham House in a huge, lumbering, old-fashioned family coach. Charlotte, with her ladies in attendance, drove from Cranbourne Lodge to War-wick House in an open carriage drawn by four bay thoroughbreds. Leopold and his gentlemen drove in two of the Prince Regent's trav-elling carriages to Hounslow, where they lunched with the botanist Sir Joseph Banks, and then, in a dress carriage drawn by six bays and preceded by outriders in livery, they drove through cheering crowds to Clarence House, where Leopold was to stay until the wedding.

At dawn on the wedding day crowds began to assemble outside Clarence House and all along the Mall between Carlton House and Buckingham House, even though the ceremony was not due to take place until nine in the evening. As if it was any other day, Charlotte spent most of the morning sitting for the sculptor Turnerelli, while friends called in as usual to pass the time with her and inspect the progress of the work.

Early in the afternoon, Leopold drove down in a curricle to Warwick House. After a brief visit with Charlotte he went back to Clarence House, where the crowd was so thick that a footman was nearly crushed to death helping him out of the curricle and several women and children were pushed in behind him as he went through the door. From then until dinner time, the calls of the crowd were so incessant and insatiable that he had to come out onto the balcony every quarter of an hour to wave.

In the evening, while Leopold held a dinner for a few gentlemen at Clarence House, Charlotte went down to Buckingham House, dined with the Queen and then went upstairs to change into her wedding dress. Outside, the escort of Lifeguards assembled, and the band of the Coldstream Guards and a guard of honour from the Grenadier Guards marched down to the courtyard of Carlton House. Inside Carlton House, guests were assembling beneath huge, hot, low-hanging chandeliers in the heavily gilded Crimson Drawing Room, where the ceremony was to be conducted by the Archbishop of Canterbury.

Just before nine o'clock, Charlotte came out of Buckingham

House, climbed into an open carriage and drove the short distance down the Mall with the Queen sitting beside her and her aunts Augusta and Elizabeth sitting opposite. 'Bless me, what a crowd', she said. She had seen the crowds that came to see the Tsar or the opening of Parliament, but she had never seen anything like the mass that had come to watch the wedding of their future Queen.

One of the guests waiting at Carlton House was Admiral Lord Keith, who was there in his official capacity as Deputy Earl Marshal. But he was not accompanied by his daughter. Before leaving Buckingham House, Charlotte sent one of her maids up to Harley Street to tell Mercer how she looked; and after the service she asked one of the guests, Princess Lieven, to do the same. But Mercer was not there to see for herself. It was said that she was not feeling well – and it may have been true. There were five bridesmaids, and the uneven number left a gap and spoiled the symmetry of the bridal procession. Perhaps there were meant to be six.

The reports that Mercer received from the maid and the Princess are not difficult to imagine. Charlotte's dress cost over £10,000. It was a white and silver slip, covered with transparent silk net embroidered in silver lamé with shells and flowers. The sleeves were trimmed with Brussels lace, and the train, which was six feet long, was made of the same material as the slip and fastened like a cloak with a diamond clasp. She wore a wreath of diamond leaves and roses, a diamond necklace and diamond earrings, both of which had been given to her by her father, and a diamond bracelet that had been given to her by Leopold.

Leopold also wore diamonds. He was dressed for the first time in his scarlet British uniform and he carried a jewel-encrusted sword that had been given to him by the Queen. Not to be outdone, the Prince Regent was dressed in the uniform of a field marshal smothered in the badges of all the honours and orders that he had had the gall to give himself.

The ceremony was short and dignified – except for Charlotte's slight giggle when Leopold promised to endow her with all his worldly goods. When it was over, Charlotte and Leopold stayed only long enough for the guests to drink their health. Then they left to change. Church bells pealed. Bonfires were lit. Field guns cracked their salute in St James's Park, and far down river the cannons at the Tower of London boomed.

Charlotte did not rejoin the guests. Instead she went straight down the private staircase from the state apartments to the courtyard, where Leopold was waiting with a few members of her family and her household. Her dress was now a simple travelling dress, but her white satin bonnet was trimmed with lace and carried a plume of ostrich feathers, and over one shoulder, in the latest fashion, in the manner of a hussar, she wore a white pelisse with ermine collar and cuffs.

Leopold handed Charlotte into their new green carriage and then climbed in beside her. Then the Queen, forgetting for a moment that they were now married, barked at Mrs Campbell to get in and ride with them as chaperone. For the only time in her life, Mrs Campbell disobeyed a royal command. The royal couple drove off alone to Oatlands, which the Duke and Duchess of York had lent them for their honeymoon.

The celebrations went on for several days, not just in London but in every town and village and every tavern throughout the kingdom. The poet laureate, Robert Southey, surpassed himself:

> From every church the merry bells rung round
> With gladdening harmony, heard far and wide
> In many a mingled peal of swelling sound
> The hurrying music came on every side.

Then he called on Heaven to bless the marriage 'with all a wife's and all a mother's happiness'. But in the last two stanzas he changed his mood discordantly and described a dark, ghostly figure who came to remind Charlotte that she would one day be Queen of England and that in the end she would be answerable to God for how she ruled her subjects.

'Hear me, O Princess,' said the shadowy form,
'As in administering this mighty land
Thou with thy best endeavours shalt perform
The will of Heaven, so shall my faithful hand
Thy great and endless recompense supply.
My name is DEATH, the last, best friend am I.'

Chapter Twenty-One

'The Perfection of a Lover'

———◆———

O N THE SECOND day of her honeymoon at Oatlands, where the 'unwholsome' air of the house was 'infected & impregnated with the smell & breath of dogs, birds & all sorts of animals', Charlotte wrote to Mercer. Leopold, she said, was 'the perfection of a lover', although she went on, 'I cannot say I feel much at my ease or comfortable yet in his society, but it will wear away I dare say, this sort of awkwardness.'

It would have been difficult not to feel awkward on a honeymoon that was anything but private. Although they did their best to keep out of the way, Leopold was accompanied by Baron Hardenbroek and Dr Stockmar, and if Charlotte had not resisted her father's pressure, she would have been accompanied by Mrs Campbell as well.

Fortunately, however, Charlotte did have Mrs Louis with her. Her trousseau, which had been made by Mrs Bean of Albermarle Street as well as Mrs Triand, contained thirty dresses and seventeen bonnets and caps, but most of the dresses needed to be altered before Charlotte could wear them. There was so much for Mrs Louis to do that 'a girl' had to be brought up from the village to help her.

The privacy of their honeymoon was also disrupted by 'a <u>very unexpected & undesired</u>' visitor. On only the second day, soon after Charlotte had written to Mercer, the Prince Regent suddenly appeared. To Charlotte's relief, he was 'in good humour'. He said nothing that was 'disagreeable' or 'unpleasant'. Instead he sat down and subjected Leopold to a two-hour dissertation on the uniforms of 'every regiment under the sun' – 'the cut of such a coat, cape, sleeve, small clothes &c..' Although Charlotte and Leopold had barely contributed to the conversation, she heard later from both her aunt Mary and from Mrs Campbell that her father had been '<u>delighted</u> with his visit'.

Next day Charlotte met Stockmar for the first time. As he admitted candidly in his diary, he was not particularly impressed by her, but the opening of his entry for that day reveals the extent to which his opinion was soon revised.

> I saw the Sun for the first time at Oatlands. Baron Hardenbroek was going into the breakfast room. I followed him, when he suddenly signed to me with his hand to stay behind; but she had already seen me, and I her – 'Aha! docteur,' she said, 'entrez.' She was handsomer than I had expected, with most peculiar manners, her hands generally folded behind her, her body always pushed forward, never standing quiet, from time to time stamping her foot, without however losing my countenance. My first impression was not favourable. In the evening she pleased me more. Her dress was simple and in good taste.

From the outset Charlotte made it plain to Stockmar that she liked him and enjoyed his company. She was soon calling him 'Stocky' and introducing him proudly to every distinguished visitor, and before long, as the entries in his diary reveal, he was as devoted to her as any of her staff.

After little more than a week, Charlotte and Leopold went up to

London, to Camelford House, where they began to receive a tedious series of 'loyal addresses' from various city councils and guilds. The first was from the Lord Mayor of London, who was received incongruously by the new bride in black because the court was in mourning for the Empress of Austria. But now that Charlotte was mistress of her own house she was in a position to receive anyone she pleased, and in the mornings, before the official engagements began, there were frequent visits from Cornelia Knight.

On 16 May they drove through huge crowds to Buckingham House, where the Queen gave a reception in their honour for over two thousand guests. Next day they received visits at Camelford House from Charlotte's uncles the Dukes of York, Clarence and Gloucester, and then they went round to call on the Duchess of York and thank her for lending them Oatlands.

Yet, despite their inevitably crowded social calendar, Charlotte and Leopold found time to indulge their shared interests in music and, above all, theatre.

After leaving the Duchess of York, they went on to Drury Lane to see the great Edmund Kean in his latest tragedy, *Bertram*. The visit to the Duchess had delayed them so much that they arrived well after the performance had started. As they sat down in their box, the audience interrupted the play with hisses and shouts of 'Stage Box!'. Leopold was taken aback: he thought they were being criticised for coming late. But Charlotte explained that this was what the audience did when they wanted a royal party to move their chairs forward so that they could see them better. So Leopold and Charlotte did as they were asked. That night and for ever afterwards, they sat well forward in their box, and the audiences were soon noticing how often the uninhibited Princess sat with her hand resting on her husband's arm.

A week later they went to the theatre again, this time to Covent Garden to see *The Jealous Wife*. As they entered the Prince Regent's box, several minutes before the performance was due to start, the curtain suddenly rose and the entire company sang the national anthem with a few additional verses which had been written hurriedly for the occasion and did not quite fit the cadence of the tune.

> Long may the Noble Line,
> Whence she descended, shine
> In Charlotte the Bride!
> Grant it perpetuate
> And ever make it great;
> On Leopold blessings wait
> And Charlotte his Bride.

A fortnight after that, Charlotte and Leopold were due to attend a performance of *Macbeth*, in which the ageing Mrs Siddons had agreed to make one last appearance. But when the day came Charlotte was in bed suffering from what Dr Matthew Baillie, the King's Physician Extraordinary, described as 'a severe cold', which had come on suddenly and forced her to leave in the middle of a charity concert a few days earlier.

Charlotte remained in bed for a week, although she was well enough to receive visits from the Queen and her aunts and uncles, and soon after that she was again going to the theatre and dinner parties.

✻

On 3 July Charlotte gave an important dinner party of her own, to which she invited the Duke of Wellington and his staff. When her father heard about it, he reverted to his old self. So far he had shown nothing but goodwill towards his daughter and her husband. Five weeks earlier he had invested Leopold with the Orders of the Garter and the Bath. But the thought of Charlotte playing hostess to the nation's greatest living hero reduced him to childish jealousy.

The Regent instructed Lord Castlereagh to give a dinner for the Cabinet on the same evening and invite Wellington to attend. When he received the invitation, Wellington declined politely, saying that he was already engaged on that evening. When the day came, however, the Regent sent a messenger to Wellington ordering him to join him at Lord Castlereagh's dinner. Wellington had no choice but to obey the royal command. So he sent his staff to dine with Charlotte and Leopold, and as soon as he could after dinner, without being rude to his host or disobedient to the Regent, he left Castlereagh's house in St James's Square and went up to Camelford House to join them. Charlotte was flattered. 'I like him of all things', she told Mercer. 'His little short, blunt manner is not at all against him, I think, when once known.'

Three days later Charlotte was suddenly taken ill at the opera. She was well enough to go to church next day, but on the day after that Dr Baillie ordered complete rest. A week later, to universal relief, she was seen out taking the air in her carriage. But on 22 July she was not well enough to attend the wedding at which her former suitor the Duke of Gloucester was married to her aunt Princess Mary.

For a while Dr Baillie was not sure what was wrong. It was possible that the Princess was suffering from the irregular menstruation that sometimes happens in the first few weeks of marriage. But by the end of the month he was ready to announce 'that H.R.H.'s indisposition arose from her having been in a state which gave hopes that she would, in a few months, have the happiness of giving birth to a Royal heir'.

The newspapers were sad about the miscarriage, but not despondent. The Princess was young and healthy. On 8 August they were glad to report that she had been seen out again in her carriage. Three days later they reported that she had held a musical evening, at which she had sung a German air in honour of her husband.

On the day after the musical evening, Charlotte wrote to Mercer, who was in Scotland. The bachelor Duke of Kent had been among her guests, and she was delighted to report that he wanted to 'get rid of' his apartments in Kensington Palace. His long-standing French-Canadian mistress, Julie de St Laurent, was very fond of their magnificent house in Ealing, but she disliked London. As a result the apartments were hardly ever used, and their 'very fine & spacious rooms' were exactly what Charlotte wanted. She had already looked at '6 houses at least' and none of them had been any better than Camelford.

She also reported that she had seen 'the Glosters'. 'They seem very comfortable & happy', she wrote. 'He is much in love & tells me he is the happiest creature upon earth. I won't say she does as much, but being her own mistress, having her own house & being able to walk in the streets all delights her in their several ways.'

At the end of the letter, however, Charlotte allowed herself a little dig that showed how much she was falling under the influence of her husband's opinions. 'Flahaud is gone to Scotland. He has been at Woburn for some days where they were the gayest of the gay, dancing, masking & God knows what all. I hope you won't see him.'

Charlotte's next letter to Mercer was written, not from Camelford House, but from Claremont. On 23 August the servants and furniture went down from London in stagecoaches and military wagons. Next day Charlotte and Leopold went down in their green carriage. As they drove towards the gate in time for dinner, the bells of the village church pealed out in greeting.

Two days later Charlotte wrote to Mercer:

With what widely different feelings to any I ever experienced in my life before, did I quit London this year, & with how little regret. I am so perfectly happy, & every day & hour have I to thank you for being so actively accessory in securing to me that wh. I now enjoy in so great a degree. What makes it more delightful is that our mutual affection as grown by degrees, & with the more intimate acquaintance & knowledge of each other's dispositions & characters;

wh. therefore will ensure us permanent domestic comfort, as our attachment has founded itself upon too firm & rational a basis for it to be overthrown.

CHAPTER TWENTY-TWO

'The House that Never Prospered'

———

I F CHARLOTTE AND Leopold were not already in love by the time they went to live at Claremont, they were certainly deeply in love soon afterwards. Each had married for selfish reasons. Leopold was ambitious, and Charlotte was the most eligible woman in Europe: she would one day be Queen of England, and he would be her consort. For her part, Charlotte was desperate to be free from her family, and Leopold was the handsomest refuge available. But they were both eager to make it work, in the course of their first few weeks together they found that they had more in common than they expected.

'Except when I went out to shoot', wrote Leopold later, 'we were together always, and we <u>could</u> be together, we did not tire'.

They read to each other, they played duets on the piano together, they walked in the park together, they drove together. But they did not ride together – Charlotte no longer rode, partly because the doctors did not think it was wise, and partly because Leopold did not approve of it. As she put it, '<u>He does not much like a ladies riding</u>, he thinks it too violent an exercise.'

They even checked their expenditure and paid bills together, despite having several people whose job it was to do that for them. Once, when Cornelia Knight came down to visit them, she halted in a doorway for fear of disturbing them because they were both at a table engrossed in piles of paper. 'Come in, come in!' shouted Charlotte, ''tis only Mr and Mrs Coburg settling their accounts.'

Charlotte enjoyed making a regular habit of little affectionate rituals like combing Leopold's hair or folding his cravats, and to please her Leopold grew a moustache, a continental adornment, still rare in England, which Charlotte had loved ever since she saw one on her favourite and much missed uncle, the late Duke of Brunswick.

Within two months of their arrival at Claremont, Stockmar wrote in his diary, 'In this house reign harmony, peace and love – in short everything that can promote domestic happiness. My master is the best of all husbands in all the five quarters of the globe; and his wife bears him an amount of love, the greatness of which can only be compared with the English national debt.'

Vice-Admiral Sir Henry Hotham, the man who prevented Napoleon from escaping to America after Waterloo, recorded that Leopold's English equerry, Sir Robert Gardner, told him, 'if he had been asked when he had observed domestic happiness approaching the nearest to perfection he should, with the most scrupulous adherence to truth, have pronounced it to have been at Claremont'.

In the tranquillity of their country estate, Leopold tried to teach Charlotte to behave more like a proper princess, with composure and dignity. But it was a course of study which both master and pupil approached light-heartedly and lovingly. Leopold's most frequent method of instruction was simply to whisper 'doucement, cherie, doucement', each time Charlotte became too loud or animated; it was a lesson that soon bore fruit, although the most immediate result was that Charlotte's first nickname for him was 'Doucement'.

Only a week after Stockmar had compared Charlotte's love with the national debt, he was recording Leopold's success.

> The Princess is extremely active and lively, astonishingly impression-able and nervously sensitive, and the feeling excited by a fleeting impression can often determine both her opinion and her conduct. Association with her husband has, however, had a markedly good effect on her, and she has gained surprisingly in calmness and self-control, so that one sees more and more how good and noble she really is.

There were some, including satirists and cartoonists, who said that Leopold had to be strict in order to control his wilful wife. But Leopold always denied this. Many years later he wrote to his niece Queen Victoria, 'I know that you have been told that she ordered everything in the house and liked to show that she was mistress. It was not so. On the contrary, her pride was to make me appear to my best advantage and even to display respect and obedience when I least wanted it from her.'

With the exception of the cynical Princess Lieven, all the visitors to Claremont were impressed by the relaxed, harmonious atmosphere. And during the first few months there were many visitors. These included the Regent, who expressed his satisfaction at the noticeable change in his daughter's demeanour, and the Gloucesters, the other newlyweds, who to Charlotte's ill-concealed irritation came to stay at their own invitation.

When the Gloucesters had gone, Charlotte wrote to Mercer:

> The Glosters have just this moment left us, & the Duke of Cambridge, nothing can have gone off better than the visit, & tho' they are not the most agreeable people in the world, still they are exceedingly good humoured, good natured, kind, & easily to be pleased... The Duke seems very fond of Mary & to be very happy;

he is certainly all attention to her, but I <u>cannot</u> say she looks the <u>picture of happiness</u> or as if she was much delighted with him.

In the next paragraph, however, Charlotte expressed very different feelings about the Duke and Duchess of York, who had come over from Oatlands to dine while the Gloucesters were staying. 'I cannot tell you what a pleasure it is to us having Oatlands so near. We like her so much...'

Then, in the last paragraph, she wrote, 'Have you seen the pamflets upon the divorce? they were sent to me.'

The only disturbances in Charlotte's new-found tranquility were the rumours that her father was again planning to divorce her mother. Old hands, like Brougham, were, as usual, taking advantage of the situation, but, although most people still wanted to support the Princess of Wales, the stories that were now leaking out made it more and more difficult to sympathise with her.

Just over two years earlier, after learning a little bit more about the Princess of Wales, Jane Austen expressed what was now becoming a more general opinion when she wrote, 'Poor woman, I shall support her as long as I can, because she is a Woman, & because I hate her Husband... But if I must give up the Princess, I am resolved at least always to think that she would have been respectable, if the Prince had only behaved tolerably by her at first.'

Political pamphlets, dealing with the constitutional consequences of a divorce, were not the only publications which featured Charlotte's mother, and one of the most sensational of the others, *The Journal of an English Traveller; or Remarkable Events and Anecdotes of the Princess of Wales*, also found its way to Claremont. In it, the anonymous author purported to list some of Princess Caroline's most indecorous escapades and describe the efforts of her husband's agents to find witnesses who would testify to them.

It was said that the Princess of Wales was now very fat and wore a black wig, that she danced with her servants, and that she had had her portrait painted naked from the waist up. And it was also said that the tall, dark, handsome, young Italian whom she had engaged as a courier to organise her journeys, Bartolomeo Pergami, was now her lover. Apparently she enjoyed making love with him in unusual places, such as in a moving carriage and in a tent on the deck of a Sicilian ship while sailing from Tunis to Greece.

There was no knowing how much or how many of the stories were true, but the more reliable reports in the letters of those who saw Caroline were disturbing enough. Lady Bessborough, daughter of the first Earl Spencer and sister of the famously beautiful Georgiana, Duchess of Devonshire, described, 'a short, very fat elderly woman, with an extremely red face (owing I suppose to the heat) in a girl's white frock-looking dress, back and neck quite low (disgustingly so) down to the middle of her stomach; very black hair and eyebrows, which gave her a fierce look, and a wreath of light pink roses on her head.'

Nevertheless, while the Prince Regent and his agents tried in vain to collect enough evidence to convince the Whig press, let alone a court, public opinion was still so much against him that his carriage was stoned in the streets of London. If Charlotte and Leopold had gone up to town, they would undoubtedly have been cheered with equal enthusiasm. But they did not go. They were more than happy to stay out of the limelight. They even cancelled the public engagement that must have been closest to their hearts. They had agreed to be the patrons of a new theatre, and they were due to lay the foundation stone on 14 September, but when the day came, to the disappointment of the dwindling crowd, the ceremony was performed by one of the City Aldermen instead.

The theatre, named after its patrons 'The Royal Coburg', opened in 1818. It had a sumptuous interior with a unique 'looking-glass curtain', which reflected the entire audience when lowered. But it survived only by producing lurid melodramas, and in 1833 a change of name to the Royal Victoria did nothing to make it more successful. In 1871 it reopened, again unsuccessfully, as a music hall, the New Victoria Palace, and ten years later a social reformer, Emma Cons, turned it into the strictly temperance Royal Victoria Hall and Coffee Tavern, where she presented concerts and excerpts from operas and plays by Shakespeare. In 1912, however, after Cons' death, the building was inherited by her niece, Lilian Baylis, who restored it to the purpose that its original patrons had envisaged. Known by the name that survives to this day, the Old Vic, it became the first theatre in the world to perform the entire canon of Shakespeare's plays.

At the beginning of December Charlotte and Leopold went to stay with other members of the royal family at her father's pavilion in Brighton. She did not feel well before she left Claremont, and the journey made her feel so much worse that she was unable to join the rest of the party for dinner when she arrived. But she was able to appear at dinner every evening after that, if only because 'everybody kept their own hours' and she had nothing to do all day but stroll around the town with Leopold. On their first outing they were so heavily jostled by an eager crowd that every day after that they had their carriage following, so that they could get away if necessary.

On 16 December, after their return to Claremont, Charlotte was well enough to hold a large dinner party to celebrate Leopold's birthday. Next day they gave a servants' ball, which was attended by as many servants as could be spared from Oatlands as well, and at which, Charlotte told Mercer, 'I never saw people enjoy themselves more.'

Christmas Eve was spent at Oatlands, where the Duchess of York held 'a sort of fete & fair for everyone'. 'It was the gayest & prettiest sight I ever saw', wrote Charlotte. Everybody 'great and small' was there – the houseparty, neighbours, servants and their children. They were all given presents, and in keeping with a charming German custom that Leopold's nephew Albert was one day to make popular throughout the kingdom, there was a little pine tree decorated with baubles and candles.

On 7 January, Charlotte's twenty-first birthday, the Prince Regent gave a ball at the Royal Pavilion. But, again, Charlotte did not feel well, and this time she could not even manage the journey. While others danced and drank her health in Brighton, Charlotte spent her birthday at Claremont, where all the villagers of Esher, whose houses were decorated with garlands, came up to the house at nightfall and stood beneath rows of torches and lanterns listening to the band that played on the lawn.

By now Charlotte's bouts of sickness were arousing suspicion. Many gossips and journalists inferred that she had suffered another miscarriage. But better suspicions were aroused and strengthened in the course of the next four months, during which Charlotte hardly ever ventured beyond the gates of Claremont.

Then, on 30 April, Leopold drove up to London and called on the Prince Regent at Carlton House. They had not wanted to say anything until they were sure. But now they were. Charlotte was over three months pregnant.

Chapter Twenty-Three

'A Brunswick Heart'

Two days after Leopold's visit to the Prince Regent in London, on 2 May, he and Charlotte gave a ball at Claremont to celebrate their first wedding anniversary. Almost all the leaders of London society came down for it. The Foreign Secretary and Lady Castlereagh were there, the Russian Ambassador and Princess Lieven were there, and so too was the newly created Marquess of Anglesey, who had commanded the British cavalry at Waterloo and was unable to dance because he had left a leg there.

Another of the guests from London was the Hon. Margaret Mercer Elphinstone. It was her first visit to Claremont. But her reception was not quite as it used to be at Warwick House or Windsor. In the past, no matter who else was there, Mercer had always been shown straight in to be with the Princess the moment she arrived. This time, however, to her obvious discomposure, she was asked to wait in line with the other guests and take her turn at being received by her host and hostess.

A few weeks later, Mercer married Count Flahault. Charlotte and Leopold were not there.

Charlotte left Claremont at least once during the summer. On 12 August she went over briefly with Leopold to Richmond to attend the party given to celebrate her father's birthday by the grandmother of another famous cavalry commander, the Dowager Countess of Cardigan. For most of the time, however, she was content to live as she had always lived at Claremont, receiving occasional visits from friends and giving dinner parties for her neighbours.

Yet despite her seclusion, Charlotte's name was seldom out of the newspapers. Every rumour about her condition, every anecdote, however unlikely, was seized upon gratefully and elaborated in print by every editor and commentator. It was all part of a happy, hopeful story – the only member of the royal family that anybody cared about was soon to give birth – and in 1817 it was almost the only happy story.

The rest of the news was always bad. Britain was in the middle of a post-war recession. Manufacturers had reduced production and laid off some of their workers. A very bad harvest had had the same effect in the country. The Corn Law, which was passed to keep the price of corn at a profitable level for farmers and landowners, had put the price of bread beyond the pockets of even those labourers who were still employed.

Charlotte and Leopold had been doing what they could, distributing food and employing as many men as they could afford to make aesthetic 'improvements' to their park. But there were not too many who did the same. Bitter indignation and resentment were widespread. Riots were frequent. The Habeas Corpus Act had been suspended so that the government, which had no effective coordinated policies, could lock up suspected rabble-rousers without trial.

At the end of August, Stockmar recorded that Charlotte's condition was even influencing the Stock Market. 'Bets for enormous sums have been made on the sex of the expected child, and it has been already calculated on the Stock Exchange that a Princess would only raise the funds 2 ½ per cent, whilst a Prince would send them up 6 per cent.'

The optimism of the press and the market was not always shared by those who saw Charlotte, however. Lady Holland described 'strange abnormal symptoms'. Several people said the Princess was so large that she was likely to have twins, and the Queen, who had as much experience of pregnancy as almost anyone, said that 'her figure was so immense (to me not natural) that I could not help being uneasy to a considerable degree'.

Before setting out on a visit to Rome, Lady Ashbrook, who had grown close to Charlotte while they were both on holiday in Weymouth, called at Claremont and strongly recommended that she should engage Sir William Knighton as 'accoucheur'. Knighton was a highly qualified physician who had studied at Aberdeen and Edinburgh. He had been made a baronet by Charlotte's father, whom he had attended on a number of occasions, and he was widely regarded as by far the best 'accoucheur' in England.

When Lady Ashbrook returned from Rome, however, she discovered to her impotent anguish that Sir William had not been appointed. Dr Baillie, who, as the King's Physician Extraordinary, was to be in charge of Charlotte's confinement, had chosen his own brother-in-law, Sir Richard Croft, instead.

Croft was fashionable but not impressive. After first meeting him Stockmar described him as 'a long, thin man, no longer very young, fidgety, and good-natured; seems to have more experience than either learning or understanding'.

Besides Baillie and Croft, there were to be two other members of the team. One of them, the nurse, was to be Mrs Griffiths, who had thirty years' experience of midwifery, and who, unlike most members of her profession in the era before Florence Nightingale, could be recommended as 'a respectable woman'. The other, the consultant, was to be Dr John Sims, a 68-year-old botanist and physician, who was said to have some expertise in the use of instruments, and who was ready to be summoned if any artificial assistance seemed necessary.

Naturally Dr Stockmar was also invited to join the team. But he refused. To have said yes would have been to push himself 'into a place in which a foreigner could never expect to reap honour, but possibly plenty of blame'. He wrote:

> I knew the hidden rocks too well, and knew that the national pride and contempt for foreigners would accord no share of honour to me, if the result were favourable, and, in an unfavourable issue, would heap all the blame on me. As I had before at various times, when the physician was not at hand, prescribed for the Princess, these considerations induced me to explain to the Prince that, from the commencement of her pregnancy, I must decline all and any share in the treatment.

Baillie and Croft had estimated that the Princess would give birth on 19 October, and at the end of August preparations began with the arrival of Mrs Griffiths. When she was introduced to Charlotte and Leopold, they came into the room as they always did, arm-in-arm, and stood talking to her 'in the most affable manner for half an hour' without ever letting go of each other.

Mrs Griffiths was given a room on the top floor, and Leopold's dressing room, which led off the bedroom, was equipped with a small bed for Sir Richard Croft, so that he would be close at hand when he was needed. As yet no arrangements had been made for Dr Sims. That could be done later if he had to be called. And there was no need to provide accommodation for Dr Baillie. Since he lived nearby at Virginia Water, he could drive over every day, and he could come quickly enough in the night if he was summoned.

Sir Richard Croft arrived two weeks after Mrs Griffiths and at once subjected Charlotte to a strict regime which, among other things, was designed to reduce her weight. The accoucheur replaced her usual and favourite luncheon, a mutton chop and a glass of port, with no more than tea and toast. He gave her purges. He bled her regularly.

Dr Stockmar was amazed and appalled. This 'lowering treatment' might still be fashionable in England, but it was no longer regarded as even sensible in Europe. 'I gave the Prince a long lecture', he wrote, 'and intreated him to make my observations known to the physicians of the Princess'. But whether Leopold did or not has not been recorded.

As Charlotte grew weaker with the regime, she began to have little bouts of gloom. She told Leopold that she thought she might die, and she did not want to see the new clothes that had been made for her baby. She had chosen them eagerly from patterns and samples, but when they arrived she had them put away without looking at them. It was as though she thought it might be bad luck if she did, and it was not something that the experienced Mrs Griffiths had ever seen a mother do before.

For the most part, however, life at Claremont went on as usual. At the beginning of October Sir Thomas Lawrence came down to paint Charlotte's portrait and stayed in the house for over a week. Charlotte wanted to wear stays when she sat for him, but Sir Richard refused to allow it. He was not always wrong, although there was no need to make his veto so indelicate. 'A cow does not wear stays', he said. 'Why should the Princess Charlotte?'

Sir Thomas was delighted by life at Claremont and by the Princess, whom he had not seen since she was a child, and who, he noted, was no longer 'boistrous'. In the mornings, when she sat for him, Leopold came with her and stayed for most of the session. In the early afternoon she drove round the park, 'in a low phaeton with her ponies, the Prince always walking by her side'. After that, until it was time to change for dinner, she came with Leopold to sit for him again. After dinner, which was attended by the whole household, Charlotte and Leopold always left the table before the others;

and, when everyone else went into the drawing room for coffee, Charlotte and Leopold were always at the piano, 'often on the same stool', playing duets or singing together.

When the newspapers reported that Sir Thomas Lawrence had left Claremont and returned to London, they still expected that, as the doctors had predicted, the Princess would give birth on 19 October. But 19 October came and went and all that they could say was that the Princess was still in the best of health and driving out daily in her little phaeton.

The Queen was waiting for news at Windsor, hoping to visit Charlotte and her baby as soon as possible after the birth. But she had not been well for some time and on Saturday, 2 November, she went down to take the waters at Bath.

By then the Prince Regent had gone to stay with his mistress Lady Hertford and her husband at Ragley Hall in Warwickshire.

Next day, Sunday, Charlotte went for a drive with Leopold, attended the service which Dr Short conducted for the entire household in the chapel and then went out for another drive.

On Monday, when the labourers returned to work on the 'improvements' in the park, Charlotte drove down with Leopold to inspect their progress on the home farm and the 'Gothick Temple'.

At around seven o'clock in the evening, the contractions began. As Charlotte climbed into the big bed that stood between the windows beneath a tall chintz canopy, she made a promise to Mrs Griffiths. 'I will neither bawl nor shreik.'

Horses were saddled and grooms stood ready to ride off and summon the Privy Councillors who were required to be present as 'witnesses' at a royal birth.

The contractions continued: sharp, soft, painful, but not yet effective. Sir Richard Croft and Mrs Griffiths stood by the bed. Leopold was there as well.

At midnight Charlotte began to feel nauseous. At 3.30 Croft decided that it was time to send for the witnesses. One groom galloped across to Virginia Water to fetch Dr Baillie. The others headed off into the dark towards London.

At 5.15 the first to arrive was the Secretary of State for War and the Colonies, who lived in Putney. The next, at 5.45, was the Home Secretary, who lived in Richmond. The Archbishop of Canterbury, who was staying with the Bishop of London in Fulham, because it was closer than Lambeth, arrived at six o'clock. The last were the two who lived in central London: the Chancellor of the Exchequer, who arrived at 7.30, and the Lord Chancellor, who arrived a quarter of an hour later.

Dr Baillie, despite living at Virginia Water, no further away than Richmond, only just made it before the Lord Chancellor.

The witnesses and Dr Baillie assembled in the breakfast room, which stood beside the bedroom and led into it through a large, thick door on the other side from Leopold's dressing room. There was nothing to report, and there was nothing to be heard. Apart from their own whispers, the only sounds were the discontented chattering and occasional squawk from Coco, Charlotte's parrot, whose stand was in the corner.

Down in the village, the gentlemen of the press, who had heard the news from the witnesses' servants, began to assemble at the Bear.

In the bedroom at Claremont, Charlotte's sporadic contractions continued ineffectively throughout the day. By seven o'clock in the evening she was tired and hungry. She had had no sleep for thirty-six hours and nothing to eat for twenty-four. But pain and Sir Richard would allow her neither. Sometimes she walked up and down in front of the fire, leaning on Leopold's arm. Sometimes she lay on the bed. Sometimes Leopold lay beside her. And sometimes she reached out and absent-mindedly played with his hair, as though no one else was there.

In the breakfast room, Dr Baillie, who had not yet been allowed to see the patient, received regular reports, reassuring him that all was going well. But at ten o'clock Croft came out, took him into the bedroom and told him that he might need to use forceps.

A groom was sent galloping up to London to fetch Dr Sims. He arrived at 2 a.m. on the following morning.

At 8.15 Croft and Sims came into the breakfast room and informed the witnesses that the Princess was making good but gradual progress and that they now hoped it would not be necessary to risk the use of forceps.

The hours went by. But now Charlotte was always in bed.

At around six o'clock in the evening, meconium, a child's first faeces, which usually appear after birth, oozed out onto the sheets. It was the first sign that the baby was in distress.

In the course of the next three hours Charlotte gave birth to a boy. He was, as suspected, dead. The doctor and the accoucheur tried every trick they knew to revive him. They plunged him in a bath of warm water. The rubbed him with mustard. They rubbed him with salt. But it was to no avail.

Charlotte had kept her promise. She had neither bawled nor shrieked, and now, heartbroken and exhausted after fifty hours of labour, she kept it still. She bore it all, said Baillie, 'with a Brunswick heart'. While Mrs Griffiths and the maids around her wept, it was Charlotte who tried to comfort them.

At 9 p.m. the witnesses were informed that Her Royal Highness the Princess Charlotte had been delivered of a still-born son. In keeping with custom, Mrs Griffiths carried in the little corpse for their inspection.

Charlotte was still bleeding. Her uterus had not fully contracted after the birth. It was now shaped like an hour-glass, and it looked as though it was not going to contract any further. Rather than wait for the placenta to be expelled naturally, Croft and Sims decided to remove it by hand. When that was done, apparently successfully, the bleeding stopped.

At last Charlotte was given some nourishment – chicken broth and toast washed down with barley water. She was also given camphor julep to stimulate her heart, and soon afterwards she became animated and began to chatter a little hysterically.

Mrs Griffiths, who had been awake and in the same dress for three days and two nights, went away to wash and change.

'How smart you are, Griffiths', said Charlotte merrily when she returned. 'Why did you not put on the silk gown, my favourite?'

Two hours later, when they had been reassured that the Princess was doing well, the sad and weary witnesses went home. Leaving Charlotte to sleep and Mrs Griffiths to watch over her, everyone else in the house went to bed.

Leopold went first to his study, to write a note telling his father-in-law what had happened. Then he went to a bedroom, lay down fully clothed and fell into a very deep sleep. He was miserable, but he was also exhausted, and it seems likely that Stockmar had given him a sedative.

Just after midnight, Charlotte felt sick. Her pulse was racing and there was ringing in her ears. She vomited and brought up the camphor julep with the broth. Then she quietened for a few minutes and her pulse-rate lowered. And then she clutched her stomach and cried out, 'Oh, what a pain! It is all here!'

Mrs Griffiths rushed into the dressing room and woke Sir Richard Croft. When he reached Charlotte moments later Croft found that she was very cold and breathing with difficulty, and she was bleeding again. But, although the accepted and often successful treatment for a post-partum haemorrhage such as this was the application of cold water, Croft decided to warm the patient up by applying hot water bottles and blankets to her abdomen. The bleeding continued.

Croft then sent a footman to bring Baillie and Sims. Baillie decided that what the Princess needed was a good dose of wine and brandy. While he was administering them, Croft went off in search of Stockmar.

Stockmar woke to find Croft holding his hand. The Princess was in danger. The Prince must be told.

Stockmar dressed and went to wake Leopold, but the Prince was so deeply asleep that it took time to wake him, and then he was so drowsy that he barely understood what was being said.

After about a quarter of an hour a footman came. Dr Baillie wanted Dr Stockmar to see the Princess. For a moment Stockmar hesitated. He was reluctant to get involved. Then he went.

When he entered the bedroom, Baillie was still trying to administer wine. The Princess was tossing from side to side, breathing heavily and obviously in great pain.

'Here comes an old friend of yours', said Baillie.

Charlotte stretched out her left hand, grabbed Stockmar's and pressed it 'vehemently'. 'They have made me tipsy', she said.

While he held her hand, Stockmar surreptitiously took her pulse. 'It was very quick; the beats now full, now weak, now intermittent.'

After another quarter of an hour there was a rattle in Charlotte's throat. Stockmar went off to get Leopold. But as he crossed the breakfast room he heard Charlotte shouting beyond the closed door behind him: 'Stocky! Stocky!'

Stockmar went back. Charlotte did not see him. She turned on her face, drew up her knees to her chest and fell silent. Stockmar took her cold hand and searched for a pulse. There was none. 'The flower of Brunswick' had faded. 'The Daughter of England' was dead.

Stockmar went to break the news to Leopold but, when at last he had woken him, he did it, by his own admission, 'in no very definite words'.

Leopold was still very drowsy. As he and Stockmar made their way to the bedroom, he sank into a chair in the breakfast room. He still thought Charlotte was alive. He asked Stockmar to go in and see how she was. Stockmar humoured him and went. Then he was blunt. 'I came back and told him it was all over.'

Leopold went into the bedroom and knelt by the bed. He took

Charlotte's cold hands in his and kissed them – 'those beautiful hands which at last while she was talking to others seemed always to be reaching out for mine'.

For a while he stayed there. Then Lieutenant-General the Prince Leopold of Saxe-Coburg-Saalfeld, who had sat impassive in the saddle through half a dozen military engagements, who had led a cavalry charge in one of the largest and longest battles in the history of Europe, stood up, turned, put his arms round Stockmar and whispered, 'I am now quite desolate. Promise to stay with me always.'

CHAPTER TWENTY-FOUR

'A Serious Misfortune'

LEOPOLD WAS NEVER the same again. Almost fifty years later he told his niece Queen Victoria that he had 'never recovered the feeling of happiness' that 'blessed' his short life with Charlotte. He had always been renowned for his reserve, but, as anyone who had ever been to Claremont knew, there was a warmth beneath it. Now, in his grief, he seemed to be more morose than reserved, and the warmth beneath was replaced for ever by a loveless chill.

On the day of Charlotte's funeral Stockmar wrote to one of Leopold's former tutors in Coburg, 'Life seems already to have lost all value for him, and he is convinced that no feeling of happiness can ever again enter his heart.'

Each day during the week that followed his bereavement, Leopold walked round and round the park in the rain with Dr Short, clutching a miniature of Charlotte in his hand. Late every evening, he went into the bedroom where Charlotte was lying and sat with her for most of the night. In Charlotte's sitting room, her watch was found on the mantelpiece, and the cloak and bonnet that she had been wearing on her last drive were still hanging on the end of a screen.

Leopold gave orders that they were to stay where she had left them.

He was inconsolable, and his pain grew greater with almost every visitor. On the day after the deaths the doctors came back to carry out a post mortem, interfering with the bodies of his wife and son in a futile search for a cause of death. Worse, Sir Everard Home, Sergeant Surgeon to the King, came to take out their guts and embalm them.

When the medical men had done their work, the undertakers wrapped the child in linen and put him in a simple open coffin. His little heart, which the doctors had taken out, was put separately into an urn. Then Charlotte, also wrapped in linen, was lifted into her own coffin and covered with blue velvet. Leopold watched, and Mrs Campbell watched Leopold. She described him that evening in a letter to Lady Ilchester. 'It was grief to look at him. He seemed so heartbroken.'

Even some of the visitors who came to comfort Leopold only added to his misery. The Duchess of York drove over from Oatlands and was so overcome with grief herself that she collapsed in the hall and had to be taken home before she saw him.

The Prince Regent came down and asked to see the bodies. He had left Warwickshire for London soon after he heard that his daughter was in labour, but the rider carrying less welcome news had somehow managed to gallop past his carriage and its escort in the dark. He was back at Carlton House and in bed when the Duke of York came to tell him that his daughter and grandson were dead. His response was uncharacteristically selfless. 'What is to be done for the poor man?' he said, falling back onto the pillow. 'Great Heaven!'

Leopold gave the Regent a lock of Charlotte's hair. Next day, the Regent's sister Princess Mary, who was now Duchess of Gloucester, took the lock, entwined it with a lock from their youngest sister, Princess Amelia, who had died in 1810, and had them made into an eternity ring for him.

The Queen, accompanied by her daughter Princess Elizabeth,

was dining with the Mayor and Corporation of Bath when the bad news reached her. She set out at once for Windsor. But back in the castle with her spinster daughters and her sad old husband she was overwhelmed with a sense of helplessness and bitter disappointment. Despair destroyed what was left of her health. It declined rapidly from that moment on. Within a year she was dead.

In Holland the Prince of Orange wept at the news, and out of deference to his grief his Russian Princess ordered the ladies of his court to dress in mourning.

When the news reached Italy, it was said, Lord Byron threw open the windows of his apartment in Venice and let out an anguished scream that was heard echoing down the Grand Canal.

Lady Charlotte Bury, who was also in Italy, summed up the situation precisely in her journal. 'There is now no object of great interest in the English people, no one great rallying point round which all parties are ready to join... A greater public calamity could not have occurred to us; nor could it have happened at a more unfortunate moment.'

In a nation still sunk in economic depression, the focus for hope had been taken away. But for the time being the people were still united, although it was only grief that united them. Public buildings were draped in black. Everyone who could afford it was dressed in black. Even the most destitute unemployed labourers were wearing ragged black armbands. Every place of worship, whatever the religion, prepared to hold a memorial service. Shops, most of which still displayed the portraits of Charlotte and Leopold that had been put there for their wedding, closed for business and then, when they opened again, filled their windows with mementoes – glass, pottery, porcelain, pewter, all engraved or crudely painted with Charlotte rising through an escort of angels to take her place in the heavenly palace. A fund was established to pay for a fitting marble memorial, and the poor were as eager to contribute as the rich: among the long list of 'subscribers' there is an unnamed child who gave sixpence.

The national grief and sentimental melancholy were unprecedented. No monarch, no minister, no national hero had ever been so deeply mourned as 'the Beloved Princess'.

✻

On 15 November Charlotte's heavy state coffin was delivered to Claremont. It was made of mahogany, studded in gold and covered in crimson velvet. The little Prince's coffin was similar, with silver studs instead of gold. The simple inner coffins were placed inside them. The urn containing the child's heart was wrapped in velvet.

In the early evening of 18 November a black carriage drawn by six black horses set off down the drive for Windsor carrying the little Prince and his heart. Charlotte followed in a hearse drawn by eight black horses with tall black plumes. Leopold rode in the carriage behind, accompanied only by Dr Short.

They were escorted by a squadron of the 10th Hussars. At Egham the Hussars were relieved, and the escort for the rest of the journey was provided by the Royal Horse Guards. It was late and dark when they arrived in Windsor. While Charlotte was installed in Lower Lodge, her son was laid in his temporary resting place in the Royal Vault in St George's Chapel. When the short service was over, Leopold went down to the lodge and spent the rest of the night, as usual, sitting beside Charlotte.

Next day Charlotte lay in state at Lower Lodge. At eight o'clock in the evening her heavy coffin was carried up to St George's Chapel by eight Yeomen of the Guard, one of whom injured his spine under the strain and died soon afterwards. Leopold walked behind them, his solemn face streaked with tears. Behind Leopold came the Royal Dukes of York, Clarence, Cumberland and Sussex. Behind the Dukes came the Cabinet, then the Archbishops, the Bishops, the officers of state and all the members of the royal households. On either side, in front of huge silent crowds, their path was lined by foot guards and lit by the burning torches that were carried by every fourth guardsman instead of a reversed musket.

The Prince Regent was not there. Nor was the Queen. He was moping in Carlton House, and she and her sobbing daughters were in her apartments nearby in the castle, listening to the bells and the muffled drums.

The service, which was disrupted at the outset by a few squabbles over seating, lasted until eleven o'clock. When it was over, Leopold waited in the deanery until the congregation had dispersed. Then he went down with Dr Short and stayed praying for a long time in the Royal Vault, where his wife and son were to remain until the tomb and the memorial that the people were buying for them were ready.

In the weeks that followed, Leopold lived alone and inconsolable at Claremont. On 16 December Sir Thomas Lawrence came down to deliver the finished portrait of Charlotte. When they saw it, the entire household burst into tears. Leopold, said Lawrence, 'was greatly affected' and spoke to him in 'that low subdued voice that you know to be the effort at composure'.

In his precise English accent, the Prince lamented:

> Two generations gone. Gone in a moment! I have felt for myself, but I have felt for the Prince Regent. My Charlotte is gone from this country – it has lost her. She was good, she was an admirable woman. None could know my Charlotte as I did know her! It was my happiness, my duty to know her character, but it was my delight!

※

Meanwhile, public sorrow evolved into recrimination. The press blamed the Queen and the Prince Regent for not being with Charlotte when she died, although, had they known it, Charlotte had said that she did not want them at the birth. They blamed the doctors, and some of the doctors blamed themselves. Sir Richard Croft, who may already have been contemplating suicide, wrote to Stock-mar, 'May God grant that neither you nor any connected with you may suffer what I do at this moment.'

And then the press turned to speculation. Who would inherit the throne of England when all the King's children were dead? The brothers and sisters could follow each other in succession for a while, but when the last of them was gone, who would succeed? There was no next generation. Perhaps the Prince Regent would divorce Char-lotte's mother, marry again and have another child. If not, they said, it was the duty of his bachelor brothers and spinster sisters to marry and have legitimate children of their own. The old King had dozens of grandchildren, some said as many as fifty-seven, but Charlotte had been the only one who was not a bastard.

An article to this effect, arguing in particular that it was the duty of the Duke of Kent to marry, appeared in the *Morning Chronicle*, and early in December a copy of that edition found its way onto the table in Brussels where the Duke of Kent was having breakfast with Julie de St Laurent.

The Duke was now living abroad in order to avoid creditors, which was why he had not been able to attend Charlotte's funeral; it so happened that, during the previous year, he had discussed his fi-nancial difficulties with Charlotte and Leopold on one of his visits to Camelford House. Since Leopold had just been granted a generous annuity by Parliament, and since the Prince Regent and the Duke of York had received similar grants when they were married, Charlotte had suggested that the Duke of Kent should follow their example, and Leopold had joined in by suggesting that he should consider his own widowed sister Victoria, Dowager Princess of Leiningen.

The Duke liked the idea. He was deeply in love and happy with Julie de St Laurent. If she had been a princess, instead of the daugh-ter of an engineer, he would certainly have married her. But, like his eldest brother, he was not a man to let love stand in the way of financial security.

Julie de St Laurent may not have realised what was happening. When her Duke went abroad briefly in the autumn of 1816, she may have been led to believe that he was making arrangements for their move to Brussels. But in fact he was visiting the Dowager Princess Victoria at her tumbledown palace in Amorbach. He spent two days with her, and when he left he wrote her a letter containing a proposal of marriage, which the Dowager Princess politely declined.

Now, prompted by the *Morning Chronicle*, the Duke of Kent wrote to Leopold, who assured him that his sister had liked him. She just felt that his proposal had come a little too soon in their acquaintance. So the Duke renewed his courtship and again asked the Dowager Princess to marry him.

This time, however, now that Charlotte was dead, there was a great deal more to his offer. As the *Morning Chronicle* had made plain, and as the Dowager Princess Victoria well knew, there was the chance of a crown in it. When the old King died, which was bound to be soon, his eldest son, the Prince Regent, would be King. If, as was more than likely, the Regent did not get divorced, marry again and have another child, he would be succeeded by the King's next son, the Duke of York; and since the Duchess of York was too old to have children, her husband was bound to be succeeded by the Duke of Clarence. For the last two years, even before the death of his mistress, Mrs Jordan, the bachelor Duke of Clarence had been searching desperately for a wife. He had proposed to almost every heiress in England, including Mercer. But so far everyone had turned him down; unless someone at last accepted him, and unless in addition he became a father, the next in line was the Duke of Kent.

Victoria was being offered a chance to fill the role that her brother Leopold had lost – consort to the ruler of England and perhaps parent to a future ruler. As long as her Duke outlived his older brothers, the only events that could destroy the dream were the births of children to the Regent or the Duke of Clarence; while the first seemed very improbable, the second was at least unlikely. It was a gamble worth taking. This time Victoria said yes.

With great dignity, Julie de St Laurent went off to live with her sister in Paris. The Duke of Kent and the Dowager Princess of Leiningen were married in accordance with Lutheran rites in Coburg on 29 May 1818. On 13 July they were married again in an Anglican service in the drawing room at Kew Palace.

By then, however, each of them had met with a disappointment. The marriage had not been as financially rewarding as the Duke had been led to expect. Parliament had long since lost patience with the royal family. 'The Princes', said the Duke of Wellington, 'are the damnedest mill-stone about the necks of any Government that can be imagined'. From now on, any Royal Duke who married was to get an extra £6,000 a year and that was all.

As for the new Duchess, she discovered that the marriage had not brought her quite as close to her dream as she had hoped. The Duke of Clarence had found someone to marry him – Princess Adelaide of Saxe-Meiningen.

The Kents' second ceremony at Kew was a double wedding. In what others saw as a charming demonstration of brotherly love, the Dukes of Clarence and Kent, both of them more than fifty years old, were married together in a joint Anglican ceremony, at which, for the sake of the brides, the order of service was printed on one side of the page in English and on the other in German.

After the ceremony, the two couples went up to the royal bed-chamber to visit the Queen, who had only four months left to live, and then, after 'a sumptuous banquet', the Duke and Duchess of Clarence went to St James's Palace and the Kents set out for Claremont, which Leopold had lent them for their honeymoon.

At the last possible moment, at the starting gate, the Duchess of Clarence had replaced the Duchess of Kent as favourite in the race to provide an heir for the House of Hanover.

Although the odds were longer, however, there were others in the field as well. Beyond the Duke of Kent there were three younger brothers.

The middle of the three, the Duke of Sussex, had married Lady Augusta Murray in contravention of the Royal Marriages Act and had therefore been withdrawn from the running, but the other two were both eligible and entered. In 1815 the elder of the two, the Duke of Cumberland, had married the widowed Princess of Solms, who was hated by the rest of the Royal Family because she had once jilted the Duke of Cambridge. Since then she had borne her husband a stillborn daughter, and although some said she was now too old, she was known to be trying for another child.

The youngest in the field, the outsider, was the man she jilted, the Duke of Cambridge, who had actually been first out of the gate. He had proposed to, and been accepted by, Princess Augusta of Hesse Cassel only two weeks after Charlotte's death, and they had been married two weeks before the Dukes of Clarence and Kent.

The race was on.

In the following year the favourite went briefly ahead by a nose. On 21 March the Duchess of Clarence gave birth to a daughter, Charlotte, but tragically the baby died a few hours later.

Five days after that the Duchess of Cambridge gave birth to a son, George.

Then, on 24 May, the Duchess of Kent pulled ahead by giving birth to a daughter. She was baptised Alexandrina, after her godfather Tsar Alexander, and Victoria, after her mother; and for the first few years of her life she was to be known as 'Drina'.

Three days later the Duchess of Cumberland gave birth to another George.

The future of the House of Hanover was now secure. King George III had three legitimate grandchildren. But Alexandrina Victoria, Leopold's niece, was the one who took precedence. After her father and three older uncles, she was fifth in line to the throne of England.

CHAPTER TWENTY-FIVE

Out of Favour

LEOPOLD WAS ABROAD when his niece Victoria was born. He was still morose and not yet ready, or even fit, to be seen out in society, and Stockmar had persuaded him that it would be better to travel than mope among memories at Claremont.

In March 1818 he went down to the Pyrenees for a while. In the summer, when he returned, he opened Claremont to the public and then, in September, left for Paris.

While he was in Paris, one of the many Englishmen who were living there at the time, Captain Gronow, invited him to shoot hare with him out at Saint-Germain. Leopold declined. 'I never intend again to shoot a hare', he said. 'At Claremont, one day, when I was walking with my beloved wife, we heard the cries of one that had been wounded; and she was so affected that she begged I would not hurt one of these animals in future.'

From Paris, Leopold went on to spend Christmas with his eldest brother, Duke Ernest, in Coburg, but he was so distressed by the sight of a happy festive family that he spent most of the time in his room.

In April he went to Vienna, where he bought a house for Ernest. Leopold was not yet ready to return to England. He wrote in English to Mrs Campbell, whom, he knew, was one of the few people Charlotte had loved, and who, he had hoped, was going to be the governess of his son:

> I should have already sooner have thought of returning to dear old England, but I greatly wanted quiet and retirement, fallen from a height of happiness and grandeur seldom equalled, to accustom myself to the painful task of leading so very different a life... I hope you will at the approaching more propitious weather visit Claremont sometimes, and look a little on your protections in the flower garden...

Leopold was still in Vienna when he heard that his sister was about to give birth in London. On 28 May, four days after Princess Victoria was born, he landed at Dover. 'The appearance of His Royal Highness', said *The Times*, 'is much improved since his departure from hence, yet he still looks very pale and much dejected; and having lost his moustachios contributes the more to make him look thin.'

Leopold spent the night in Dover and went home next day to Claremont. On the day after that he visited the Duchess of York at Oatlands, and on the last day of the month he went up to London, called on the Regent at Carlton House and then went round to Kensington Palace to meet his niece.

In the evening he went back to his huge new London home, Marlborough House. The house had been built by the first Duchess of Marlborough on a plot of land next to St James's Palace which she leased from her friend Queen Anne. In 1817, after Charlotte and Leopold moved into Claremont, the lease had reverted to the Crown, and the Queen and the Regent, knowing that the young couple were dissatisfied with Camelford House, had decided to give it to them.

Now Leopold was living there alone and solemnly redecorating and furnishing it, so that he would be able to entertain there when he took his place in London society again.

Mrs Campbell, who was invited round to see the house, described it to Lady Ilchester. 'The Prince has laid out a great deal of money on Marlborough House, in painting and cleaning it, very handsome carpets to the whole range of apartments, and silk furniture, and on my asking if the silk on one sofa was foreign, he seemed quite to reproach me, and said I should never see anything that was not English in his house.' But he still talked most about Charlotte, and Mrs Campbell was 'gratified' to report that 'he also told me of his parties for the next month, and who he was going to ask'.

Leopold's first appearance in society was at the banquet that followed the christening of Princess Alexandrina Victoria. He then went to the Prince Regent's birthday party, and thereafter he gave a few dinner parties and attended others. But he was still so dejected that he was a dour host, and such a dull companion at other people's tables that hostesses despaired of him. It was as much of a relief to them as to him when he went back to Claremont.

※

At the end of the summer the Duke of Kent took his wife and daughter down to spend the winter in Sidmouth on the south coast of Devon. On 20 January 1820 Leopold received a note from his sister telling him that the Duke had caught a chill and was suffering from a severe chest infection. Leopold raced down to Sidmouth and was at the Duke's bedside when he died three days later.

On 29 January the old King died.

The Prince Regent was now King George IV; eight-month-old Drina – Princess Victoria – was now third in line to the throne after the Royal Dukes of York and Clarence.

The Duchess of Kent inherited nothing but her husband's debts.

Fortunately, however, Leopold was rich. Parliament had agreed that the £50,000 a year it had voted to him on his marriage should continue to be paid for the rest of his life. Even after the 'great deal of money' he was spending on Marlborough House, he had income to spare. He paid some of the debts, made arrangements to pay off others over the next few years and assigned £3,000 a year to be spent on his niece's education. The Duchess of Kent and her daughter could go on living in Kensington Palace without any worries, and her brother would always be on hand if she needed him. Princess Victoria would never know her father, but her 'dearest Uncle Leopold', as she was soon to call him, was determined to stand in for him as much as he could.

The new King set about planning his coronation with all the ceremonial enthusiasm shown when he was Regent. But six hundred miles away, in northern Italy, other plans were being made which did not quite accord with his. Now that her husband was a king, Charlotte's mother wanted to be a queen. She announced that she was coming back to be crowned beside him in Westminster Abbey.

Brougham tried to persuade her to stay away. He had heard too much about her. He knew that she was now so grotesque that it would not be long before the press and then the people turned against her. In his opinion there was much more political capital to be made out of her if she could be presented as an innocent exile. But the Radical Whigs did not agree. They believed that they could only use her to rouse the discontented rabble if she was actually in the country to form a focus for their fury. And it was the Radical counsel that prevailed.

Fat, fifty-two and foolishly dressed in clothes that were far too young for her, Caroline, Princess of Wales, accompanied by Willikin, landed at Dover on 5 June and was cheered all the way to London by well-organised crowds. For a few days, while she lived in South Audley street with the Radical MP Matthew Wood, mobs roamed the streets breaking windows and shouting, 'God save the Queen!', but the disorder died away when she moved to take up permanent residence at Brandenberg House in Hammersmith.

The King's response was brusque and to the point. He told the government to get rid of her, and warned that he would get rid of the government if it did not.

Since the King could not divorce his wife in one of his own courts, the only way of ending the marriage was by Act of Parliament. But the appropriate Bill of Pains and Penalties could not be introduced until the government had collected enough evidence to support it. As a first step, the Queen would have to undergo a form of trial before the House of Lords. It was a project from which no one was likely to emerge with any dignity. Leopold offered to mediate. Perhaps the Queen could be persuaded to accept a compromise. But the Prime Minister refused to let him. Her Majesty had already rejected all offers. She was insisting on being crowned. The Bill of Pains and Penalties was the only option.

The trial opened on 17 August. On that day and each day that followed, the new evidence was a delight to the gossips, satirists and cartoonists. Italian witnesses were produced to substantiate almost every lurid rumour. When Brougham, who had been landed with the defence, tried to make them contradict their evidence under cross-examination, the answer that one of them kept repeating became the most popular catchphrase of the day – 'Non mi ricordo'.

After only a few days Leopold could stand no more of it. Although mobs had again started to riot in support of her, the Queen was being represented to the court as a debauched hussy, and she was adding to the impression herself by slouching in her chair and yelling abuse at the witnesses. He decided to reason with her. If she accepted a compromise now, she might at least hold on to her popular support and avert complete humiliation.

He went down to Brandenburg House. But the visit was ill-advised, futile and disastrous. His mother-in-law refused to see him, and when his father-in-law heard about it he was furious.

In his own way the King had been good to his son-in-law. He had made him a Field Marshal and a Knight of the Garter; and he had given him the title His Royal Highness. As he saw it, Leopold's visit to Hammersmith was ungrateful, disloyal and presumptuous.

The entertaining trial was allowed to run its course. But on 10 November, on its third reading, the Bill of Pains and Penalties only passed through the House of Lords by a majority of nine. The Prime Minister knew that it would never pass through the Commons. Rather than risk a defeat, he withdrew it. Instead the Privy Council ruled that, since the Queen was living separately from the King, she had no right to be crowned with him, and he could refuse to allow it if he chose. It was a solution that would have been better received if it had been used early enough to prevent the embarrassment of the trial. The Radicals claimed the climb-down as a victory, and their rabble rioted again.

The exclusion of the Queen from the coronation was at least enough to prevent the King from carrying out his threat to dismiss the government, but he was still exasperated and in no mood to forgive Leopold for interfering. When Leopold went to court a few weeks later, the King ostentatiously turned his back on him. Without any change in the expression on his face, Leopold walked up to the Duke of York. 'The King has thought proper at last to take his line', he said loudly, 'and I shall take mine.' Then he walked out.

By then the Duchess of Clarence had given birth to another daughter, Elizabeth. But the child only lived until the spring. On 19 July 1821, when Leopold set out in his garter robes to attend the coronation of King George IV, his niece Victoria was again third in line.

Out of favour though he was, Leopold had at least been invited to the ceremony in Westminster Abbey. The Queen, on the other hand, had not. In accordance with the ruling of the Privy Council, she had been specifically instructed not to come. But she insisted that it was her right to be there. She turned up in her carriage and went round the Abbey from door to door demanding to be admitted, and at every door she was turned away. When she climbed back into her carriage and drove off, for the first time, the scanty crowds booed her.

As Brougham knew they would in the end, the press and the people turned against the Queen. Now they sympathised with the satirist who wrote:

> Most gracious Queen, we thee implore
> To go away and sin no more;
> Or if that effort be too great,
> To go away at any rate.

The Queen did not go away. Instead, three weeks later, she died of bowel cancer. She probably knew that she was dying when she went to Westminster Abbey, and she may even have known for some time before that, but the first time she told anyone was when Brougham went to see her two weeks after the coronation. 'I am going to die, Mr Brougham', she said, 'but it does not signify'.

Apart from the Queen's ludicrous appearance and the abuse that the crowds shouted at their King, the coronation was pronounced a success. Mrs Campbell wrote to Lady Ilchester, 'Nothing could be finer than the sight of the Coronation, and Prince Leopold the most beautiful part of it.'

But cutting a dash in public was about all that Leopold was able to do during the next few years. Now that he was out of favour with the King, he was given no role in the world, and he remained too dull and introspective to be a success in society. George FitzClarence, who had just returned from service in India, described him as 'a damned humbug'. The only people who sought him out were the many mothers, including Lady Augusta Murray, who tried in vain to interest the rich and handsome Prince in their daughters.

Leopold was not celibate, however; he had several mistresses, among them the beautiful Countess Ficquelmont and the notorious Lady Ellenborough, who, in character though not in shape, was very like his mother-in-law. But he was so cold, so completely incapable of tenderness, that they all left him for other lovers.

His only human interest lay in the education and welfare of his niece Victoria. She alone inspired his affection. He arranged holidays for her in Weymouth, and as often as possible he took her down to Claremont with her mother. In 1872, when she had been Queen for thirty-five years, Victoria wrote, 'Claremont remains as the brightest epoch of my otherwise melancholy childhood.'

On 7 Jan 1827 the Duke of York died. The Duke of Clarence was now heir to the throne, and Victoria was heir presumptive. But as Victoria's destiny drew closer, Leopold became more and more dissatisfied with his own lack of achievement. He was thirty-seven years old, and all he had to show for it was a good war record and the fact that he was the uncle of a future Queen. He did not even have a family.

There had been a spark of hope back in 1825, when the Greeks sent a deputation to London to invite Leopold to be their king. But the Greeks' proposal depended on their unlikely success in freeing themselves from the Ottoman Empire, and it did not have the support of George Canning, the new Foreign Secretary.

Canning had taken office when Castlereagh committed suicide after being caught by a blackmailer in a bedroom with a boy dressed as a woman. In his opinion the offer was too far-fetched to be taken seriously, and anyway Leopold was likely to be more useful if he stayed in England. The King was not in good health, and nor were his brothers of York and Clarence. The imminent death of all three was a much more likely eventuality than the freedom of Greece. If that did happen within the next few years, England would be left with an infant Queen, and in that event her uncle would be an ideal regent.

In July 1827, however, Canning, who was by then Prime Minister, died from the chill that he caught at the Duke of York's funeral; on 20 October, in the last great battle fought between wooden warships, Admiral Codrington inadvertently destroyed the Ottoman fleet at Navarino.

Greece was within grasp of independence. The offer was renewed. Leopold was inclined to accept, and this time he had the support of no less a person than the Duke of Wellington. But the vengeful King was opposed to the plan, and the King's opposition was enough to thwart it.

When Leopold's frustration evolved into bitterness, Stockmar decided that it was time to go travelling again.

Chapter Twenty-Six

The Hottentot

I N September 1828 Leopold's travels took him to Prussia, to Potsdam, where he stayed in the palace as the guest of King Frederick William III.

One evening, in the King's private theatre, the State Company gave a performance of a popular musical comedy, *The Hottentot*. When the 21-year-old actress who played the title role came on, wearing a short red frock trimmed with tiger skin, coral trinkets and a black and white feathered headdress, Leopold was enraptured and astonished. She looked just like Charlotte.

Her name was Caroline Bauer, and she had just returned from a triumphant season in St Petersburg. Her late father had been an officer in the Baden Light Dragoons. Her mother, who had been born a Stockmar in Coburg, was the aunt of the little doctor who was sitting out in the auditorium in the row behind Leopold. Her family had, of course, disapproved of her ambition to become an actress, but when it became clear that they could not stop her, her cousin, Dr Christian, had agreed to help, on the whimsical condition that she would always wear new shoes and new gloves at each performance.

Caroline Bauer knew that Leopold was in the audience. When she looked out through the peep-hole in the curtain before the performance began, she was able to recognise him easily. He was the 'slender, tall gentleman, in red English uniform glittering with gold, of pale, noble face, with short, black, smooth-lying hair, and great, dark, melancholy eyes'.

When the performance was over, Caroline went home with her mother, who, in true theatrical tradition, accompanied her everywhere. On the following morning a valet came to inform them that Prince Leopold intended to call on them next day.

When the Prince came, he came in a hired carriage, rather than use his own and risk being recognised by the livery and the coat of arms on the doors. But he was not so cautious when he began to talk. The restraints of the last eleven years were cast aside impulsively.

First, according to Caroline's memoirs, he told her mother why he had come. 'All the long years since the death of my consort, I have been living alone. Now I believe I have found the sympathetic creature I have been looking for. At the very first glance my heart was drawn to her, because she looks so wondrously like my departed Charlotte.'

Then, not many minutes later, he asked Caroline what she would do if he were to ask her to share his 'golden solitude'.

If Caroline or her mother were embarrassed by his words, she did not say so in her memoirs. The Prince was offering marriage. It was to be a morganatic marriage, in which the wife could not share her husband's rank and the children could not inherit his possessions or his titles. But it was marriage. Caroline and her mother said yes.

A few days later mother and daughter drove to Coburg. They were met by cousin Christian and taken first to the Duke's country estate at Rosenau, where a fair was being held on the lawn. Caroline was encouraged to join in the dancing, and while she was waltzing with a young farmer she looked up at the terrace in front of the house. The Duke and his two young sons, Ernest and Albert, were standing on it watching the dancers, and his brother Leopold was beside them, searching for Caroline through a telescope.

Next day mother and daughter were installed in a pretty country house, where, in the presence of Stockmar, Leopold renewed his promise to marry Caroline. He was off to Italy for a while, but when he returned to England he would lease one of the new houses in Regent's Park and send for them.

Leopold may not have taken in too much of Italy in the course of the next few months. He was certainly so preoccupied that he overlooked his most cherished duty. One of the letters that he received while he was there ended with a complaint from Kensington Palace. 'I am very angry with you, Uncle, for you have never written to me once since you went.'

In May 1829, after he had returned to England, Leopold kept part of his promise and sent for Caroline and her mother. As they drove up from Dover in an open carriage, Caroline was impressed by the condition of the English roads and the rich farms that surrounded them, and when they reached London she was astonished by the number of shop windows that were still displaying the portraits of Charlotte and Leopold which had first been hung there twelve years earlier.

The terraced house in Regent's Park was beautiful. The ground floor contained a saloon with a fine grand piano in it, a dining room, a billiard room and a boudoir for Caroline with pink silk walls and curtains; and upstairs, among the bedrooms, there was a bathroom lined with blue and white tiles. But when Caroline and her mother arrived, the only person there to meet them was the German housekeeper, who had tea ready.

Next day they waited. At last, in the evening, Leopold arrived. He had not seen Caroline Bauer for eight months, but all that he could say when he did, and not with admiration, was, 'Oh, how the spring sun has burnt your cheeks!'

Leopold stayed for an hour, and every day after that the ritual was the same. He came in the afternoon and stayed for an hour or two, just listening to Caroline reading or playing the piano. Sometimes he brought sheet music with him, so that she could play something new, and every time he brought his tortoise-shell drizzling-box.

Drizzling was then a fashionable hobby. It involved taking the gold and silver epaulettes and frogging from old uniforms, putting them into a little box, turning a handle and grinding them into a dust which, when melted, became precious metal again. Leopold was so fond of drizzling that he had already produced enough silver to make a soup bowl for his niece Victoria, and he was soon to produce enough to make her a tureen.

By the end of June, Stockmar had become as exasperated with this as his aunt and cousin. He confronted Leopold. He told him that the King of Prussia had written to ask whether Fraulein Bauer was his mistress or not, and he warned him that, if he did not make an honest woman of her, she would have to be taken home. He knew that the Prince was doing nothing but drizzling while Caroline read or sang to him, but that was not what other people thought he was doing.

On 2 July 1829, in the saloon of their house in Regent's Park, Leopold and Caroline formalised their relationship. It was not a marriage. There was no priest present. It was not even a morganatic marriage. All that happened was that they signed a contract, witnessed by Stockmar and his brother Charles, in which Leopold promised to pay Caroline a small annual allowance for the rest of her life.

After that, for the rest of July, they were happy. They were together by day and they were together by night. Somehow Leopold's heart lightened and his spirits lifted. 'It was', wrote Caroline, who could never be anything but theatrical, 'the last youthful flicker of his burnt out heart before it finally crumbled for ever into cold ashes'.

At the end of the month, after a merry farewell dinner, Leopold went off to take the waters at Carlsbad, in the hope that they might help his recurring rheumatism, Stockmar went off to Coburg, where he now had a wife, and Caroline and her mother went off happily to spend a few weeks in Paris.

But Leopold did not join them in Paris until the middle of November, and when he got there he booked into a different hotel. The old routine returned. Every afternoon Leopold came round for an hour and sat drizzling while Caroline read to him.

Early in December Leopold went back to England accompanied by Stockmar. But it was not until after Christmas that Caroline and her mother were brought over and installed, not in the terraced house in Regent's Park, but in a drab little villa with brown carpets and old furniture on the edge of Claremont Park. Leopold's sister and niece, who were staying in the house for Christmas, were often there at other times as well, and as it would not have been appropriate for them to meet, it seemed better to lodge Caroline and her mother elsewhere.

The drizzling routine continued, but at least now it did not happen every day. The negotiations over Greece were on again, and this time there was more chance of success. The King was now so sick that he might not have the energy to object. Leopold was often in London, and when he was away and there were no guests in the house, Caroline and her mother were allowed to wander around Claremont like tourists.

On one occasion, in Charlotte's sitting room, they found her cloak and bonnet still on the screen, and her watch still on the mantelpiece, and in the breakfast room they found a nervous and neglected parrot covered in lice with half his grey feathers missing. He was Coco. When Leopold returned, Caroline asked if she could take the parrot and nurse him back to health. Without a glimmer of emotion, Leopold gave him to her.

On another occasion Caroline noticed a portrait of Charlotte dressed in a traditional blue and silver Russian costume, which had been given to her by the Grand Duchess Catherine. Caroline's theatrical wardrobe contained one almost exactly like it. Hoping to warm

Leopold's heart by reminding him of her likeness to his Princess, she wore it for him next time he came round for a drizzle. But, after the initial and inevitable surprise, his only response was to make comparisons. Charlotte had a more finely cut nose. Caroline's mouth was prettier. Charlotte had a fuller figure. Caroline was more graceful. But the colour of their hair and their complexions were identical...

When the pedantic inventory was finished, all that crestfallen Caroline could do was to remind the Prince of the one attribute he had forgotten. 'Your Highness forgets the faithful hearts which beat, or have beaten, for you.'

Leopold was on edge again. The negotiations over Greece had given him a goal, but the frustration and tension that had been eclipsed briefly by the happiness of last July had returned. He was grinding his teeth so much in his sleep that, against Stockmar's advice, he bought a pair of little gold clamps. According to the quack who made them, these would keep his teeth apart all night if he inserted them on either side between his molars before he went to bed. But after only a few nights he woke to find that the clamps were gone. Believing that he had swallowed them, the dignified Prince asked Stockmar to give him the most powerful purge that he could make, and it was only after he had taken it that a servant discovered the clamps amid his sheets.

In February Leopold accepted the throne of Greece. For a while his spirits lifted as he planned his future. He ordered some beautiful blue and white tents which he intended to use when he travelled round his kingdom. He subjected Caroline to the humiliation of discussing who he might have as his queen. But when he thought about it more, he was not sure that he had made the right decision. Greece, although free, was far from stable, and the greatest barrier to his ambitions, the King of England, was clearly on the brink of death. Perhaps destiny had something better in store for him. In May he changed his mind and declined the Greek throne.

By then Caroline had had enough. Like the other mistresses

before her, she was exasperated by Leopold's indifference. She began to indulge in fits of overwrought theatrical indignation, and she wrote to her brother Karl in Germany complaining bitterly about her treatment.

There is no record of exactly what happened next. All that is certain is that Karl came over and subjected Leopold to some sort of blackmail. Stockmar stepped in to negotiate, and at the beginning of June, probably after receiving a payment, the Bauer family went back to Germany.

Caroline returned to the stage and continued her successful career until 1844, when she retired to marry a Polish count. Coco, now healthy and happy, went with her, learned to speak German and died while they were on tour in Dresden in 1842.

Soon after the Bauers' departure, on 26 June, the King died. The Duke of Clarence was now King William IV, and eleven-year-old Victoria was heir to the throne.

At last the future looked brighter for Leopold. The King who had stood in his way had gone and, as the recent Greek offer had shown, there were many statesmen in Europe who respected him enough to present him with opportunities. There were to be moments in the course of the next few years when he felt that his life might have been easier if he had chosen to spend it in the sun, but he could not regret rejecting Greece because he knew now that he could do better. If the new King died before Victoria came of age, the government might even make him Regent.

He was right not to regret Greece. But his reason was wrong. Destiny had something different in store for him.

King of the Belgians

———◆———

A FEW WEEKS after the death of King George IV there was another revolution in France. The totalitarian King Charles X had appointed a reactionary Cabinet, dissolved the Chamber of Deputies and imposed censorship on the press. In response, the citizens of Paris took to the streets. After overwhelming the inadequate garrison, they drove the King into exile in Scotland and replaced him on the throne with his distant cousin the Duke of Orleans, who was crowned as King Louis-Philippe.

When the news spread across the northern border, into the province that had until recently been known as the Austrian Netherlands, the people of Brussels poured out onto their own streets and gleefully followed the French example.

Their province had been conquered by the French in 1795, just before Charlotte's mother set out for England, and in 1815, at the suggestion of the British government, it had been incorporated into the United Kingdom of the Netherlands by the Treaty of Vienna. Since then, however, the new Dutch King, William I, the father of Charlotte's first fiancé, had been almost as repressive as the King of

France. Although the French-speaking, Roman Catholic Belgians in his new province outnumbered the Protestant Dutch by almost two to one, he had not given them even equal representation in the upper house of their parliament: he had subjected them to the rule of Dutch civil servants, he had forced them to speak Dutch in the law courts and he had imposed heavy taxes in order to pay off the Dutch national debt. But he had not occupied the province with enough soldiers to hold down a rebellion. On 4 October 1830, the Belgians declared their independence.

King William appealed for help to the Russians, Austrians and Prussians. But the Russian army was busy putting down a rebellion in Poland, and the Austrians and Prussians would not fight without the Russians. Instead, all three sent representatives to a conference in London, where the incomparable British and French representatives, Lord Palmerston and Prince Talleyrand, persuaded them to recognise an independent Belgium and even guarantee its neutrality.

The constitution of the new nation was modelled on the constitutional monarchy of Great Britain, and at first it was suggested that the throne should be offered to the Prince of Orange. But when the Belgians, not surprisingly, rejected Slender Billy, it was offered to Leopold. Leopold said yes, and the Belgians said yes to Leopold.

Before leaving England, Leopold gave up his house in London and his annuity of £50,000, although he persuaded the government to go on paying the donations which he and Charlotte had made to various charities. But he could not bear to part with Claremont, and it was agreed that the house should be his for the rest of his life.

Leopold left for his new kingdom at the end of June 1831. Almost immediately he was involved in a war. On 2 August Belgium was invaded by a large Dutch army under the command of the Prince of Orange. The Belgian army was no match for it. It was small, ill-equipped and barely trained. Defeat was inevitable. But Leopold had powerful allies. When a French army marched into Belgium and a British fleet appeared off the coast, the Dutch invaders fell back.

Yet, despite the unassailable strength of Leopold's supporters, it was not until 19 April 1839, almost eight years later, that the Dutch at last recognised an independent Belgium; at the same time the five Great Powers formalised their London agreement, in the treaty that was to be dismissed so famously by the German Kaiser in 1914 as nothing more than 'a scrap of paper'. The Prince of Orange, who had hoped that at least his Russian brother-in-law would continue to support him, was bitterly disappointed. Soon afterwards he said of Leopold, 'There is a man who has taken my wife and my kingdom.'

Since a king must have a queen, if only to bear him heirs, Leopold looked round for the most useful candidate and chose twenty-year-old Princess Louise-Marie, eldest daughter of his most powerful neighbour, King Louis-Philippe of France. They were married in a combined Roman Catholic and Lutheran service on 9 August 1832.

Queen Louise-Marie soon lost her youthful exuberance and became a dull, dutiful and dignified wife. She bore four children – three sons, the first of whom died within a year, and one daughter, whom she allowed without argument to be christened Charlotte. Although her husband was more than twice her age, she always adored him. But she was under no illusions. She knew that his English Princess was the only woman he had ever loved, just as her children always knew that their father cared more for his niece Victoria than he ever did for any of them.

Leopold wrote regularly to Victoria, advising her on every aspect of her conduct and education while she was a princess, and on every aspect of statecraft while she was a queen.

When she was still a princess he once composed a long essay for her on the reign of the irresolute and impressionable Queen Anne. In reply Victoria thanked him for telling her 'what a Queen ought not to be' and hoped that he would soon tell her 'what a Queen ought to be'.

If Leopold sent a second essay, it has not survived, but throughout his life, in many of his letters, he often turned to the same example of how a princess ought to be. In 1845, on Queen Victoria's twenty-sixth birthday, he sent her as her present a portrait of this 'noble-minded and highly gifted' example. At the end of the letter that went with it he wrote, 'Grant always to that good and generous Charlotte – who sleeps already with her beautiful little boy so long – an affectionate remembrance, and believe me, she deserves it.'

By then Uncle Leopold's influence with the Queen was even greater than it had been when she was a princess. In the spring of 1837, when it seemed likely that King William IV was dying, Leopold sent Stockmar to live at Claremont and instructed him to help and advise his niece in every way he could. On 20 June, one month to the day after Stockmar landed, the King died. Next day, the Queen wrote in her journal, 'Saw Stockmar.' Within two years, rooms had been set aside permanently for Stockmar's use in Buckingham Palace and Windsor Castle.

After his influence over the English court, Leopold's greatest family interest lay in arranging influential marriages. He was so success-ful at it that the Prussian Chancellor Bismarck described the House of Coburg as 'the stud farm of Europe'. By the time his own children came of age he had already arranged marriages for five nephews and, of course, a niece.

In 1836, shortly after he married his nephew Ferdinand to the Queen of Portugal, Leopold told his eldest brother, the dissolute Duke Ernest, to take his two sons, Ernest and Albert, to London to visit his sister in Kensington Palace and introduce them to their cousin Victoria. At the time Victoria was not much impressed by either of them. But when she met Albert three years later at Windsor she wrote to her uncle, 'Albert's beauty is most striking, and he is so amiable and unaffected.'

Leopold's niece and nephew Victoria and Albert were married on 10 February 1840. It was the most influential of all the marriages that he arranged. But just over eight years later, his own marriage suddenly ceased to be influential, or even useful. There was another revolution in Paris. On 24 February 1848 his father-in-law Louis-Philippe abdicated. Unconvincingly, but somehow successfully, the French King and his Queen disguised themselves as Mr and Mrs Smith and escaped to England, where Leopold had arranged for them to live at Claremont.

By the end of the year Louis-Napoleon, the son of Queen Hortense and her husband King Louis of Holland, had been elected President of France. Four years later, after a coup d'état, he was enthroned as the Emperor Napoleon III.

If Leopold ever wondered whether the Emperor knew about his relationship with his mother, he was left in no doubt a few years later, in 1854, when he went to visit him in Calais, in a vain attempt to prevent the French and the British from attacking the Russians in the Crimea. The Emperor received him on a ship called *La Reine Hortense*, and as soon as he had greeted him he thanked him pointedly for being so kind to his mother when the allies occupied Paris in 1814.

Louis-Philippe did not live long enough to see himself replaced by another Emperor. He died at Claremont on 26 August 1850. Two weeks later his daughter Queen Louise-Marie died of a broken heart in Ostend.

Leopold took easily to being a widower. He went on living very much as he had lived before. He had had mistresses before his wife died, and he went on having them, even though he was in his sixties and wore a black wig. He had worn the wig for some time, not to hide a bald patch, and not to hide any grey hair, which, like many of his contemporaries, he could have done more easily with dye, but because, so he said, it kept his head warm. Over the years his vanity and his hypochondria had grown in equal proportions together.

As he had done before, he went on arranging marriages, and when the time came he arranged them for his children. His son and heir, Leopold, Duke of Brabant, was married to Marie-Henriette, the daughter of the Archduke Joseph of Austria. It was not a happy marriage. Within four weeks of her wedding she wrote, 'If God hears my prayers, I shall not go on living much longer.' But she did live, and she bore her brutal husband two daughters – Stephanie, who married the Austrian Crown Prince Rudolf, who shot himself and a mistress at Mayerling, and Louise, who spent seven years in a lunatic asylum and then vanished.

Charlotte was married happily to the Austrian Emperor's brother, the Archduke Maximilian, and her younger brother Philippe was eventually married to Princess Marie of Hohenzollern.

But the superficial success of these marriages was overshadowed for Leopold by tragedy in another. On 9 December 1861 Albert died of typhoid fever. Leopold wrote long consoling letters to Victoria, some of them alluding, he thought helpfully, to how he felt when he lost Charlotte; the Queen wrote back, sometimes addressing her uncle tellingly as 'My dear father'.

Leopold went over to London for the funeral, at which the Prime Minister, Lord Palmerston, inadvertently embarrassed him by introducing him to the French Ambassador and his wife – the Count and Countess Flahault.

He was accompanied by his latest mistress, Frau Meyer von Eppinghoven. Although it fooled no one, the beautiful lady pretended to be his nurse, but as it turned out this was the only part that she was called upon to play. Leopold spent most of his time in bed suffering from pleurisy and gall-stones.

When he went home, a fortnight later than he intended, he knew that he only had a few more years to live, and only a year and a half after that his sense of doom was magnified by the news that Stockmar had gone before him. But there was still time for one more adventure, although, if he had been in better health, he might have thought twice about it, and if Albert or Stockmar had still been alive they might well have advised against it.

In 1861, in one of the last brash examples of 'gunboat diplomacy', France, Spain and Great Britain seized the port of Vera Cruz in Mexico and refused to return it until the Republican government of Benito Juarez paid all the interest on its national debt that was due to French, Spanish and British bondholders. But the French Emperor's real plan was to conquer Mexico, turn it into an empire and put the Austrian Emperor's brother Maximilian on the throne. When Palmerston found out what he was up to, he refused to have anything to do with it and withdrew the British forces. But Napoleon told the Austrians that he had agreed, and by the time they learned the truth it was too late.

Maximilian and Charlotte went out to Mexico, where she became known as Carlotta, and Leopold rejoiced in the knowledge that his daughter was an empress. But they were not wanted, and they did not have enough soldiers to impose their rule. Indeed it was only the famous gallantry of the French Foreign Legion that prevented them from being captured or expelled.

In 1865, at the end of the American Civil War, the government of the United States brought pressure to bear on the French, and it became clear that Napoleon was about to give in and withdraw his soldiers. In the following year, in desperation, Carlotta came back to Europe and travelled from court to court pleading for help. She even went to the Vatican. When the Pope told her that, like everyone else, he could do nothing, she refused to leave and spent the night in a small room watched over by two nuns, claiming that Napoleon was trying to poison her. Next day, when they brought her out, she was totally mad.

Meanwhile, in Mexico, Napoleon withdrew his troops, and Maximilian was captured and shot by the Juaristas.

Carlotta never recovered. She lived out the rest of her long life in the castle of Bouchout in Belgium, where she went on calling herself an empress and talking about her handsome husband as though he was still alive. She died at the age of eighty-six, in 1927.

During the First World War, when the German Kaiser's soldiers invaded Belgium, in contravention of the treaty that created it, a large notice was hung on the gates of the drive that led up to Carlotta's castle. 'This Castle is occupied by Her Majesty the Empress of Mexico, sister-in-law of our revered ally the Emperor of Austria. German soldiers are ordered to pass by without singing, and to leave the place untouched.'

Leopold did not live long enough to know that the Mexican adventure had ended in such tragedy. When he died at his country house at Laeken, on 10 December 1865, his daughter was still an empress.

Knowing that he was dying, he asked that his body be taken to England and buried in Windsor with his first wife and their son. He even wrote to Victoria, who agreed to it. His ministers, however, would not allow it. He was the King of the Belgians. He must be buried among his people. But they could only control his earthly remains. Gathered round the bed in accordance with tradition to witness the last moments of their king, they must have known that his heart and mind were in England, when they heard him whisper as life left him, 'Charlotte... Charlotte.'

SELECT BIBLIOGRAPHY

A NOTE ON SOURCES

The principal sources for this book are newspapers, journals, published letters, diaries and memoirs. Since almost all quotations are already identified by their source and date in the text, it seemed superfluous to identify them again by page numbers in chapter notes.

PRIMARY PUBLISHED SOURCES

Albermarle, 3rd Earl of, *Fifty Years of my Life*, 2 vols. (London, 1876)

Argyll, Duke of, ed., *Intimate Society Letters of the Eighteenth Century*, 2 vols. (London, 1910)

Aspinall, A., ed., *Letters of the Princess Charlotte, 1811–1817,* (London, 1949)

Aspinall, A., ed., *The Correspondence of George, Prince of Wales, 1770–1812*, 8 vols. (London, 1963–71)

Aspinall, A., ed., *The Letters of King George IV, 1812–1830*, 3 vols. (Cambridge, 1938)

Bauer, Caroline, *Memoirs of Caroline Bauer*, Trans. (London, 1884)

Benson, A. C. and Esher, Viscount, ed., *The Letters of Queen Victoria, 1837–61*, 3 vols. (London, 1908)

The Book, or the Proceedings and correspondence upon the Subject of the Inquiry into the Conduct of the Princess of Wales (London, 1813)

Brougham, Henry, *The Life and Times of Henry Lord Brougham written by himself,* 3 vols. (London, 1871)

Bury, Lady Charlotte, *The Diary of a Lady in Waiting*, ed. A.F. Steuart, 2 vols. (London, 1907)

Fairburn, J., ed., *An Inquirey, or Delicate Investigation, into the Conduct of Her Royal Highness the Princess of Wales* 4th ed. (London, 1820)

Glenbervie, Lord, *The Diaries of Sylvester Douglas, Lord Glenbervie*, ed. Francis Bickley, 2 vols (London 1928)

Knight, Cornelia, *Autobiography*, 2 vols. (London, 1861)

Lewis, Lady Theresa, ed., *Extracts of the Journals and Correspondence of Miss Berry from the year 1783 to 1852* (London, 1865)

Londonderry, 3rd Marquess of, ed., *Memoirs and Correspondence of Viscount Castlereagh, 2nd Marquess of Londonderry,* 12 vols. (London, 1853)

Malmesbury, 3rd Earl of, ed., *Diaries and Correspondence of James Harris, First Earl of Malmesbury*, 4 vols. (London, 1844)

Minto, Countess of, ed., *Life and Letters of Sir Gilbert Elliot, 1st Earl of Minto*, 3 vols. (London, 1874)

Murray, the Hon. Amelia, *Recollections, 1803–1837,* (London, 1868)

Quennell, Peter, and Powell, Dilys, ed., *The Private Letters of Princess Lieven to Prince Metternich* (London, 1948)

Robinson, Lionel G., ed., *Letters of Dorothea Princess Lieven during her Residence in London, 1812–1834,* 2 vols. (London, 1902)

Stockmar, Baron E. von, *Denkwurdigkeiten aus den Papieren des Frieherrn Christian Friedrich von Stockmar* (Brunswick, 1872)

Temperley, Harold, ed., *The Unpublished Diary and Political Sketches of Princess Lieven together with some of Her Letters* (London, 1925)

Wellington, 2nd Duke of, ed., *Supplementary Despatches, correspondence, and Memoranda of Arthur Duke of Wellington [1797–1819],* 15 vols. (1858–65)

NEWSPAPERS AND JOURNALS

The Morning Chronicle
The Times
The Gentleman's Magazine

SECONDARY SOURCES

Adolphus, J. H., *The Trial of Her Majesty, Queen Caroline* (London, 1820)

Aspinall, A., *Lord Brougham and the Whig Party* (Manchester, 1927)

Bridge, F. R. and Bullen, R., *The Great Powers and the European State System, 1815–1914* (New York, 1980)

Bury, J. P. T., *Napoleon III and the Second Empire* (London, 1964)

Corti, E. C., *Leopold I of Belgium,* trans. J. McCabe (London, 1923)

Creston, Dormer, *The Regent and his Daughter* (London, 1932)

Fulford, Roger, *Royal Dukes,* (London, 1933)

Fulford, Roger, *George the Fourth,* (London, 1935)

Fulford, Roger, *The Trial of Queen Caroline* (London, 1967)

Gash, N., *Lord Liverpool* (London, 1984)

Green, Thomas, *Memoirs of Her Late Royal Highness, Charlotte Augusta of Wales And Saxe-Coburg* (London, 1818)

Gronow, Captain R. H., *Reminiscences* (London, 1861–6)

Hamilton, Lady Anne, *Secret History of the Court of England, from the accession of George III to the death of George IV,* 2 vols. (London, 1832)

Hawes, Francis, *Henry Brougham,* (London, 1957)

Hibbert, Christopher, *George IV, Regent and King, 1811–1830* (London, 1973)

Hinde, W., *George Canning* (London, 1973)

Holden, A., *Uncle Leopold* (London, 1936)

Holme, Thea, *Prinny's Daughter* (London, 1976)

Huish, Robert, *Memoir of the Princess Charlotte of Saxe-Coburg* (London, 1818)

Jones, Mrs Herbert, *The Princess Charlotte of Wales* (London, 1885)

Juste, T., *Memoirs of Leopold I, King of the Belgians,* Trans. R. Black, 2 vols. (London, 1868)

Lucas-Dubreton, J., *Louis-Philippe* (Paris, 1938)

Plowden, Alison, *Caroline and Charlotte* (London,1989)

Renier, G. G., *The Ill-fated Princess* (London, 1932)

Richardson, Joanna, *The Disastrous Marriage* (London, 1960)

Smith, E. A., *A Queen on Trial* (London, 1993)

Smith, E. A., *Lord Grey, 1764-1845* (London, 1990)

Staniland, K., *In Royal Fashions* (London, 1997)

Stuart, D. M., *Daughter of England* (London, 1951)

Weigall, Lady Rose, *A Brief Memoir of the Princess Charlotte of Wales* (London, 1874)

JACKET AND PLATES

Jacket: Engraved by W. T. Fry after a drawing by George Dawe (Museum of London)

Plates: The Prince Regent, Sir William Beechey (Royal Collection)

Caroline of Brunswick (Royal Collection)

Princess Charlotte by Sir Thomas Lawrence (Royal Collection)

Claremont House by Caleb R. Stanley (Royal Collection)

Cornelia Knight by Angelica Kauffmann (City of Manchester Art Gallery)

Mercer Elphinstone by John Hoppner (Marquess of Lansdowne)

Crimson Drawing Room by W. H. Pyre (*Royal Residences,* 1819)

Charlotte by George Dawe (National Portrait Gallery)

Charlotte by Richard Woodman (National Portrait Gallery)

Leopold (Royal Collection)

Henry Brougham by J. Lonsdale (National Portrait Gallery)

Hortense by Anne-Louis Girodet-Trioson (Rijkmuseum)

Madame Récamier by Jacque-Louis David (Louvre)

'A German Present' by Williams

The Heriditary Prince of Orange by J. B. Van der Hulst (Foundation of the Historical Collections of the House of Orange-Nassau)

Leopold by Sir Thomas Lawrence (Imperial Library of Vienna)

Leopold in Garter Robes by Sir Thomas Lawrence (Royal Collection)

'To Be, or, Not to Be' by Lewis Marks

'A Brighton Hot Bath' by George Cruickshank

Every effort has been made to acknowledge correctly the source and/or copyright holder of each picture, and the publisher apologises for any unintentional errors or omissions, which will be corrected in future editions.

INDEX